VIRGINIA
WILDLIFE
VIEWING GUIDE

Mark Damian Duda

FALCON™

Falcon Press® Publishing Co., Inc.,
Helena, Montana

ACKNOWLEDGMENTS

Over 300 Virginia biologists, conservationists, managers, and educators contributed to this guide by nominating and reviewing sites, peer reviewing manuscripts for accuracy, and providing useful information. Space limitations prohibit me from mentioning each of them by name, however it in no way lessens their valuable contributions.

Karen Terwilliger, Virginia Department of Game and Inland Fisheries; Skip Griep, USDA Forest Service; and Rupert Cutler, Virginia's Explore Park, were early advocates of the guide. They contributed as Steering Committee Members as well, along with Dr. Mitchell Byrd, College of William and Mary; Scott Klinger, USDA Forest Service; Patrick McMahon, Virginia Division of Tourism; Jefferson Waldon, Virginia Tech; Keith Watson, National Park Service; and Donald West, Virginia Department of Transportation.

Significant assistance also came from John Bazuin, Jr., Virginia Society of Ornithology; Charlie Sledd, Larry Hart, Phil Smith, Spike Knuth, and Irvin Kenyon, Virginia Department of Game and Inland Fisheries; Ed Haverlack, USDA Forest Service; Dwight Stallard, Virginia Department of Forestry; Teresa Martinez and Don Owen, Appalachian Trail Conference; and Napier Shelton, National Park Service. Susan Cerulean, author of the *Florida Wildlife Viewing Guide* offered valuable materials and advice. Amy Leary and Kira Young of Mark Damian Duda and Associates, Inc. assisted in numerous ways and kept the project focused, organized, and on schedule. My wife, Mary Anne, and daughter, Madeline, accompanied me on site visits making research pleasurable and memorable.

I am especially indebted to Kate Davies, Wildlife Viewing Guide Program Manager and John Grassy, Falcon Press Editor, for their support and guidance throughout this project.

Author and State Project Manager:
Mark Damian Duda

Wildlife Viewing Guide Program Manager:
Kate Davies, Defenders of Wildlife

Illustrator:
Swannee Nardandrea

Front cover photo:
Bald Eagle, LYNN M. STONE

Back cover photos:
Big Meadows, ROB SIMPSON

Gray Fox, BILL LEA

COMMONWEALTH of VIRGINIA

Office of the Governor

The Commonwealth of Virginia has been blessed with beautiful natural resources, extraordinary historic resources, and a bounty of spectacular wildlife. Virginia is home to over 100 species of mammals, over 400 species of birds, 150 species of reptiles and amphibians, and almost 250 species of fish. This is why over one million people take automobile tours or hiking trips throughout Virginia each year—to appreciate firsthand the wealth and variety of wildlife sharing our countryside.

Enjoying this abundant diversity has now been made easier, thanks to the *Virginia Wildlife Viewing Guide.* This guide highlights 80 special places in Virginia, offering particularly good opportunities to find, observe, and enjoy wildlife. The guide also provides valuable hints on when to go, what to bring, and what you may see once you arrive.

A partnership of state and federal agencies, nonprofit organizations, and Virginia businesses helped develop this guide. On behalf of all these organizations and the citizens of our state, I welcome you to the Commonwealth of Virginia. Enjoy your visit and enjoy your viewing.

George Allen

George Allen
Governor of Virginia

3

CONTENTS

Copyright © 1994 by Falcon Press Publishing Co., Inc.,
Helena and Billings, Montana. Illustrations copyright © 1994
by Defenders of Wildlife, Washington, D.C.
Published in cooperation with Defenders of Wildlife.

Defenders of Wildlife and its design are registered
marks of Defenders of Wildlife, Washington, D.C.

All rights reserved, including the right to reproduce this book or any part
thereof in any form, except brief quotations for reviews, without the written
permission of the publisher.

Design, typesetting, and other prepress work by Falcon Press, Helena, Montana.

Printed in Korea.

Cataloging-in-Publication Data

Duda, Mark Damian.
    Virginia wildlife viewing guide / Mark Damian Duda.
        p.   cm. -- (Watchable wildlife series)
    Includes index.
    ISBN 1-56044-292-1
    1. Wildlife viewing sites--Virginia--Guidebooks.   2. Wildlife
watching--Virginia--Guidebooks.   3. Virginia--Guidebooks.
    I. Title   II. Series
    QL211.D83 1994   94-19271
    508.755--dc20   CIP

PROJECT SPONSORS

 DEFENDERS OF WILDLIFE is a national, nonprofit organization of more than 80,000 members and supporters dedicated to preserving the natural abundance and diversity of wildlife and its habitat. A one-year membership is $20 and includes subscriptions to *Defenders*, an award-winning conservation magazine, and *Wildlife Advocate*, an activist-oriented newsletter. To join or for further information, write or call Defenders of Wildlife, 1101 Fourteenth St. N. W., Suite 1400, Washington, D. C., 20005, (202) 682-9400.

 THE VIRGINIA DEPARTMENT OF GAME AND INLAND FISHERIES is dedicated to the conservation of the inland fish and wildlife resources of the Commonwealth. The Department's goals focus on providing optimum populations and diversity of wildlife species and habitats, and enhancing opportunities for the enjoyment of wildlife, boating and related outdoor recreation. The Department owns and manages more than 35 wildlife management areas totaling over 180,000 acres, over 35 public fishing lakes and nearly 200 public boat ramps. To learn more about the Department of Game and Inland Fisheries, contact us at 4010 West Broad Street, Richmond, Virginia 23230, (804) 367-1000.

 THE U.S.D.A. FOREST SERVICE manages the Jefferson and George Washington National Forests in Virginia, totalling approximately 1,640,000 acres. An unparalleled variety of wildlife viewing opportunities are available on your Virginia National Forests. The mission of the Forest Service is to manage resources to benefit the public while protecting these resources for the future. The Eyes on Wildlife Program enhances opportunities for all people to experience wildlife, fish, and plant resources and encourages the public to learn about and support conservation efforts. Jefferson National Forest, 5162 Valleypointe Pkwy., Roanoke, VA, 24019 or the George Washington National Forest, P. O. Box 233, Harrison Plaza, Harrisonburg, VA 22801.

 The NATIONAL PARK SERVICE is charged with administering the units of the National Park System in a manner that protects and conserves their natural and cultural resources for the enjoyment of present and future generations. In Virginia, the National Park Service administers over 15 units. National Park Service, 143 South Third Street, Philadelphia, PA 19106, (215) 597-7013

 VIRGINIA POWER, the eighth-largest investor-owned electric utility in the United States, is fully committed to meeting the energy needs of our 1.8 million customers in an environmentally responsible manner. We believe it is both good business practice and our duty to protect the natural resources of the communities we serve, and are pleased to sponsor this viewing guide as part of our support of environmental initiatives fostering wise use of natural resources and balanced enhancement of wildlife habitats. Virginia Power, Public Affairs, P.O. Box 26666, Richmond, VA 23261, (804) 771-4417.

 THE VIRGINIA DEPARTMENT OF CONSERVATION AND RECREATION'S mission is simple: Conserve Virginia's natural and recreational resources. DCR manages more than 65,000 acres of state parks and natural areas with conservation in mind. It does this so visitors can not only enjoy themselves, but learn to appreciate open spaces, historical, and natural treasures. Department of Conservation and Recreation, 203 Governor Street, Suite 302, Richmond, VA, 23219, (804) 786-1712.

THE U. S. FISH AND WILDLIFE SERVICE is pleased to support the Watchable Wildlife effort in furtherance of its mission to conserve, protect, and enhance fish and wildlife resources and their habitats for the continuing benefit of the American people. Programs include the National Wildlife Refuge System, protection of threatened and endangered species, conservation of migratory birds, fisheries restoration, recreation/education, wildlife research, and law enforcement. U. S. Fish and Wildlife Service, 300 Westgate Center Dr., Hadley, MA 01035, (413) 253-8200.

 THE NATIONAL FISH AND WILDLIFE FOUNDATION, chartered by Congress to stimulate private giving to conservation, is an independent not-for-profit organization. Using federally funded challenge grants, it forges partnerships between the public and private sectors to conserve the nation's fish, wildlife and plants. National Fish and Wildlife Foundation, 18th and C Street N. W., Washington, D. C. 20240, (202) 208-4051.

 VIRGINIA DIVISION OF TOURISM is responsible for promoting the Commonwealth's tourism destinations and attractions to national and international audiences through trade and consumer marketing. It publishes an annual travel guide and coordinates the publication of statewide brochures designed for specific niche markets such as golf, skiing, historic homes, the Civil War, and trail-walking. Virginia Division of Tourism, 1021 East Cary Street, Richmond, Virginia 23219, (804) 786-4484.

 THE DEPARTMENT OF DEFENSE is the steward of about 25 million acres of land in the United States; many areas possess irreplacable natural and cultural resources. The Department of Defense supports the Watchable Wildlife Program through its Legacy Resource Management Program, a special initiative to enhance the conservation and restoration of natural and cultural resources on military land. Department of Defense, Office of the Deputy Assistant Secretary of Defense (Environment), 400 Army Navy Drive, Suite 206, Arlington, VA, 22202.

The VIRGINIA DEPARTMENT OF TRANSPORTATION manages the third-largest highway network in the nation, totalling over 55,000 miles, while always exercising exceptional environmental awareness and protection. VDOT's Adopt-a-Highway Program is the second-largest in America with over 6,000 groups cleaning about 25 percent of the available roads. And for nearly 20 years, VDOT has been on the cutting edge of wetland protection by minimizing impacts and pioneering techniques of wetland restoration and banking. VDOT also provides the official Virginia state map, free of charge at all welcome centers and visitor information centers. VDOT, 1401 E. Broad Street, Richmond, VA 23219, (804) 786-5731.

CONTRIBUTORS

Southern hospitality is not a thing of the past in Virginia. Many hotels and inns graciously contributed to this project by boarding weary travelers: Anderson Cottage, Warm Springs; Bent Mountain Lodge, Copper Hill; Boar's Head Inn, Charlottesville; Fairview Bed and Breakfast, Amherst; Fort Lewis Lodge, Millboro; Graves' Mountain Lodge, Syria; Hummingbird Inn, Goshen; Inn at Gristmill Square, Warm Springs; Jordan Hollow Farm, Stanley; Langhorne Manor, Lynchburg; L'Auberge Provancale, White Post; Milton Hall Bed and Breakfast, Covington; Montross Inn, Montross; Mountain Lake Hotel, Mountain Lake; Norfolk Marriott, Norfolk; North Bend Plantation, Charles City; Renaissance Manor, Stafford; River Ridge Guest Ranch, Millboro; and Stillmeadow Inn, Franktown.

INTRODUCTION

Wildlife viewing is one of the fastest-growing recreational activities in the nation. Between 1980 and 1990, according to the U.S. Fish and Wildlife Service, there was a 63 percent increase in participation. The appeal of wildlife viewing is obvious. It takes people to unspoiled and scenic natural areas, can be done on a year-round basis, and allows people to observe the beauty of nature, which, despite the exhaustive efforts of photographers and writers, always reveals itself best on a one-to-one basis. Wildlife viewing is also a great way to teach children about the outdoors. Research indicates that the best way to foster positive attitudes about wildlife and the environment is direct participation in such activities as hiking, wildlife viewing, and bird identification.

No matter the time of day or time of year, there is always wildlife to be observed, studied, and photographed in Virginia. The Commonwealth's diversity of plants and animals, in fact, exceeds that of any other temperate area of comparable size. From the eastern shore to the Blue Ridge Mountains, the state offers spectacular viewing opportunities in every season. Spring brings warblers to Virginia, and experienced birders can challenge themselves to identify the Commonwealth's 34 species. The Lafayette River in Norfolk hosts 600 pairs of nesting yellow-crowned night herons in the summer, easily viewed from a boat. In the fall, wildlife viewers can marvel at vast flocks of migrating snow geese, or count hundreds of broad-winged hawks making their way south. Mason Neck is the winter home of 50 to 60 American bald eagles.

This guide was written to showcase some of the best places in Virginia to view wild animals in their natural surroundings. More than 150 sites were considered for inclusion, and stringent standards were used to evaluate and select the 80 viewing sites herein. Many worthy sites were not included due to space limitations; others were eliminated to protect fragile wildlife and habitats from damage.

Before visiting a site, carefully review the information presented in this guide—you'll learn about the types of wildlife found in a specific area, the optimal seasons for viewing selected species, on-site facilities, special attractions such as guided nature walks and wildlife checklists, and viewing tips designed to help you see more wildlife. Use the wealth of information presented in this guide, and your chances for a successful wildlife viewing trip will be dramatically increased.

Enjoy your explorations of the magnificent natural areas that are the Commonwealth of Virginia. May your journeys also inspire you to support the many agencies and private organizations working to protect Virginia's wildlife and wildlands for generations to come.

THE NATIONAL WATCHABLE WILDLIFE PROGRAM

The National Watchable Wildlife Program was initiated in response to sky-rocketing public interest in wildlife viewing activities and interest in the environment and out-of-doors. Over a million Virginians and tourists take trips annually in the Commonwealth for the specific purpose of watching wildlife.

The *Virginia Wildlife Viewing Guide* is part of a nationwide series of guides that showcase some of the best wildlife viewing sites in the country, and are integral components of the National Watchable Wildlife Program. The National Watchable Wildlife Program consists of: 1) A network of wildlife viewing sites, 2) A uniform system of road signs directing travelers to wildlife viewing sites, and 3) The wildlife viewing guides. Virginia's Watchable Wildlife Program consists of a partnership of state and federal agencies and private businesses working to promote ecotourism, conservation, and education in Virginia.

The partnership formed to produce this guide and wildlife viewing network will continue to work together on site enhancement, interpretation, and conservation education. Travel routes will be marked with the brown-and-white binoculars sign appearing on the cover of this book. Travelers will also notice these signs in other states. As future partnerships are formed, the United States eventually will be linked by a network of wildlife viewing sites.

Enhancement of individual sites is the next step. This will involve such things as interpretive signs, trail development, viewing blinds or platforms, and provisions for parking and restrooms. Many sites in this guide are already developed as Watchable Wildlife areas, while others provide only access at this time.

The National Watchable Wildlife Program was founded on the notion that support for wildlife is built upon experiencing first-hand the beauty, excitement, and awe that is inspired by viewing wildlife in its natural environment. As Aldo Leopold, the father of wildlife management in America, noted a half century ago, "Our ability to perceive quality in nature begins, as in art, with the pretty. It expands through successive stages of beauty to values as yet uncaptured by language."

The success of wildlife conservation in America depends upon the active involvement of citizens. Use this guide to observe, photograph, and learn more about wildlife species so that you can effectively participate in their conservation. Support agency efforts to fund wildlife diversity programs and local conservation efforts in your home town.

HOW TO USE THIS GUIDE

Your wildlife viewing guide contains a wealth of information. Please take a few moments to become familiar with its contents and organization.

This guide is divided into **6 sections**, representing the major regional divisions of Virginia. Each region opens with a **full-color map** identifying all wildlife viewing sites, along with major roads and towns. The name of each viewing site is also listed.

The written description of each wildlife viewing site includes a series of **wildlife icons** at the top of the page. These icons represent wildlife groups most commonly seen at the viewing area. Wildlife icons are identified on page 12. As you become familiar with these icons, you can quickly reference the major groups of wildlife found at every site.

The text of each viewing site includes a description and viewing information. The **description** section provides a brief overview of the habitats found at each site, and names specific species to look for. It is followed by a **viewing information** section, which includes additional species, the probability of seeing selected species, and the optimal months or seasons for viewing. Specific viewing locales within site boundaries are offered when possible. *NOTES OF CAUTION RELATING TO ROAD CONDITIONS, SAFETY ISSUES, AREA CLOSURES, AND OTHER RESTRICTIONS APPEAR IN CAPITAL LETTERS.*

Written **directions** are supplied for each viewing site. The name of the **closest town** appears beneath the directions—in most cases, this is the nearest town offering fuel and a pay phone. In all cases, viewers should supplement the directions in this guide with an up-to-date state map, road atlas, county road maps, or, in some cases, topographic maps. Viewing sites are marked with signs displaying the brown-and-white binoculars logo.

Also included in each site account is the name of the agency, organization, or corporation which owns or manages the viewing site. A **phone number** is included and may be used to obtain additional information. If there are several owners, more than one number may be present.

Recreational icons appear at the bottom of each site account. These icons are identified on page 12 and provide important information about recreational opportunities, parking, entrance fees, and restrooms.

AN IMPORTANT NOTE ON HIGHWAY INFORMATION

In this guide, the complete name of a road or highway is given in the first reference for each viewing site, with subsequent references abbreviated. Due to space limitations, however, Virginia state highways are abbreviated throughout the book:

Virginia Primary Route appears as **VA PR**
Virginia Secondary Route appears as **VA SR**

FEATURED WILDLIFE

Songbirds Perching Birds	Waterfowl	Upland Birds
Wading Birds	Birds of Prey	Marine Birds
Shorebirds	Bats	Insects
Deer	Carnivores Mammals	Small Mammals
Freshwater Mammals	Reptiles, Amphibians	Crustaceans
Fish	Wildflowers	Bears

FACILITIES ICONS

Parking	Restrooms	Picnic
Campground	Trails	Barrier-Free
Entry Fee	Restaurant	Lodging

Boat Ramp	Large boats	Small Boats	Bicycles

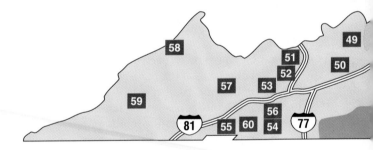

VIRGINIA
WILDLIFE VIEWING AREAS

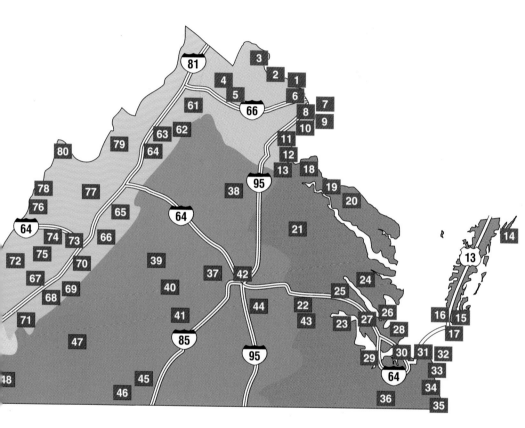

As you travel in Virginia and other states, look for these special highway signs that identify wildlife viewing sites. These
signs will help you to the viewing area. NOTE: Be sure to
read the written directions provided with each site in this
book—highway signs may refer to more than one site along a
particular route.

PLANNING A WILDLIFE VIEWING TRIP

Whether your trip will span a day or a week, advance planning will result in a more comfortable, efficient, and successful outing.

Carefully review each site account in this guide before you visit. Check for warnings about roads, seasonal closures, and available facilities.

Note the daily and/or seasonal activities of wildlife to be sure the animals you want to see are present and active. Make reservations for wildlife tours well in advance of your visit.

Consider the need for special clothing and other items for your trip. Dressing in layers is a good idea when you spend time out-of-doors. Sturdy shoes or boots are essential in more rugged country. A hat, sunscreen, and sunglasses can increase your level of comfort; polarized sunglasses can aid viewing of fish and marine life. Arrive prepared and you'll be able to stay in the field longer, increasing your odds of seeing wildlife.

Always travel with an up-to-date road atlas. Obtain a free Virginia road map by calling 800-VISIT-VA. Or purchase the indispensable DeLorme Virginia Atlas & Gazetteer, which includes 80 detailed topographic maps of the state. DeLorme maps are available in many stores.

Most Virginia travel destinations offer free information on accommodations, restaurants, campgrounds, and other attractions. Check the *Virginia Travel Guide,* published by the Virginia Division of Tourism; call 800-VISIT-VA for a free copy.

Raccoon

14

TOOLS OF THE TRADE

A pair of binoculars or a spotting scope is standard equipment for successful and more enjoyable wildlife viewing.

Binoculars come in various sizes, such as 7x35 or 10x50. The first number refers to how large the animal will be magnified compared to the naked eye. A "7x" figure, for example, means that the animal is magnified seven times. Greater magnification is not always better! A bird in a tree will be harder to find with a 10x magnification than with a 7x, because small movements, even breathing, will cause the image to move around. The second number in the couplet refers to the diameter of the lens that faces the animal. The larger that number, the greater the amount of light entering the lens—which means better viewing in dim light.

Spotting scopes on tripods are useful for viewing more stationary wildlife at long distances, such as viewing animals tending a nest.

Field guides are standard equipment, too. There are pocket-sized guides identifying virtually every plant and animal found in Virginia. Be sure to take along guides for the wildlife species you are interested in identifying.

Many wildlife watchers are interested in photographing the animals they see. For best results with general wildlife photography, use medium-speed slide film such as ASA (ISO) 100 (Fujichrome or Ektachrome) or ASA (ISO) 64 Kodachrome. For print film, use ASA (ISO) 100 or 200.

Early morning and late afternoon are the best times to photograph: animals are more likely to be active, and the rich light of morning and evening will create a better image than the harsh light of midday. Use a wide-angle lens (20-28 mm) to capture scenic shots. Use the greatest depth of field possible. Use a telephoto lens (200-400 mm) for the best close-up shots of wildlife. Allowing space between wildlife and the camera will reveal animals in a more natural pose, and place them in their habitat.

LOOKING IN THE RIGHT PLACE...

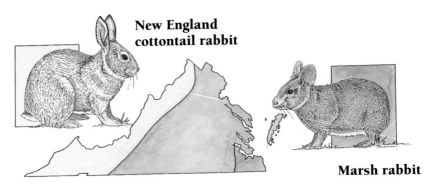

New England
cottontail rabbit

Marsh rabbit

Looking in the right place is crucial for successful wildlife viewing. Many species occur only in certain regions of Virginia. For example, the New England cottontail rabbit can be found only in western Virginia, while the marsh rabbit can be found only in the southeastern portion of the Commonwealth.

Learn to associate different wildlife species with their habitats. Every animal lives in a specific habitat, a place that provides the right combination of food, water, and cover an animal needs for nesting, hiding, feeding, and sleeping. The red-shouldered hawk, for example, prefers swampy woods where it feeds primarily on snakes and frogs. The red-tailed hawk, on the other hand, favors drier upland areas, where it feeds mostly on small rodents.

Recognizing the inextricable link between an animal and its habitat is a key not only to successful wildlife viewing, but a fundamental lesson in wildlife conservation. Without the proper habitat, a species cannot exist.

Red-shouldered
hawk

...AT THE RIGHT TIME

For successful wildlife viewing, timing is everything. You must think in terms of animal activity during the day *and* during the year. Some animals are active during the day; other species are active only at night. Animals such as owls, bats, raccoons, bobcats, flying squirrels, and opossums are active at night. Other species, including songbirds, hawks, and red and gray squirrels, are active during the day.

Red squirrel

Opossum

Some wildlife species are present in Virginia only during certain times of the year. The cliff swallows that nest in spring on the John Kerr Dam (site 46 in this guide) spend the winter in South America. The snow geese that winter in flocks of hundreds at Back Bay National Wildlife Refuge (site 34) travel to the Arctic for the summer.

Other species will be seen only at certain times of the year, not because they migrate, but because they become inactive. During winter, reptiles and amphibians become dormant; black bears hibernate through the coldest months of the year.

Each site description in this guide provides information about when many birds, mammals, reptiles, and amphibians are best seen. It's also a good idea to consult field guides for additional information about the daily or seasonal activities of the animals you want to see. Many parks and refuges have checklists available on species presence and abundance during different seasons.

Snow goose

WILDLIFE VIEWING TIPS

Kentucky warbler

Common yellowthroat

When viewing animals, learn to observe colors, markings, shape, behavior, songs or calls, and other "field marks." You'll quickly develop skill in identifying different species, as well as the difference between male and female animals. For example, although the Kentucky warbler and common yellowthroat look similar, the Kentucky warbler has distinctive yellow "spectacles." Have a field guide or two handy to aid in identifying the animals you see.

Upon arriving at a viewing site, several strategies may be used to see wildlife. The first is to stay in your vehicle and wait for animals to pass by. Many animals are accustomed to seeing vehicles, and may not feel threatened unless you try to get out. The second strategy is to find a comfortable place, sit down, and remain still. Trees and vegetation can be used as a viewing blind; you might also consider using a drop cloth of camouflage netting, or a portable blind. Another strategy is to move slowly and quietly through the area, looking and listening for wildlife. Take a few steps, avoiding brittle leaves or twigs, then stop, look, and listen. Look for subtle movements in bushes and trees. Try to isolate the call of one bird, then scan the area with binoculars to find it.

Eastern hognose snake

THE WILDLIFE WATCHER'S CODE OF ETHICS

Skink

1. Get close to wildlife using binoculars and zoom lenses.
2. Wildlife habitat must be protected; stay on marked trails.
3. Respect the rights of landowners. Get permission before entering private property.
4. Respect the rights of others viewing wildlife.
5. Do not use calls or whistles to attract wildlife.
6. Teach others, especially children, about the importance of not disturbing wildlife.
7. Never touch "orphaned" or sick animals. Young animals that appear to be alone usually have parents waiting nearby.
8. Leave pets at home; they may startle, chase or even kill wildlife.
9. Never feed wild animals.
10. Move away slowly and immediately from an animal if it stops feeding and raises its head sharply, appears nervous or aggressive, changes its direction of travel, exhibits a "broken wing" display, or circles repeatedly.

Northern cardinal

The goal of wildlife viewing is to observe and enjoy wild animals in their natural surroundings without interrupting their normal behavior. Overzealous viewers can cause serious problems for the very animals they care so much about. Too often, viewers tend to think in terms of their own behviour during a single encounter with an animal, not in terms of *cumulative* impacts. For the well-being of wildlife, however, viewers must consider the impact of all those human-wildlife en-counters that preceeded their visit, and all those that will follow.

Black bear

REGION ONE: NORTHERN

Bordered by the Potomac River on the north and east, and the eastern slope of the Blue Ridge Mountains on the west, this region contains remarkable wildlife diversity despite its close proximity to the urban sprawl of the Washington D. C. metropolis. Many of the viewing sites in this region follow the Potomac as it flows toward the Chesapeake Bay. Winter along the Potomac offers some spectacular wildlife viewing opportunities for diving ducks, bald eagles, and tundra swans. Traveling west from the Potomac the land gently rises, and urban landscapes change to open farming country and scattered woodlots. The open farmland provides excellent habitat for red-tailed hawks, blue-birds, bobwhite, white-tailed deer, and red fox. Continuing west, the land rises to meet the Blue Ridge to 2 additional wildlife viewing sites, Sky Meadows State Park and the G. R. Thompson Wildlife Management Area.

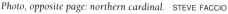

Photo, opposite page: northern cardinal. STEVE FACCIO

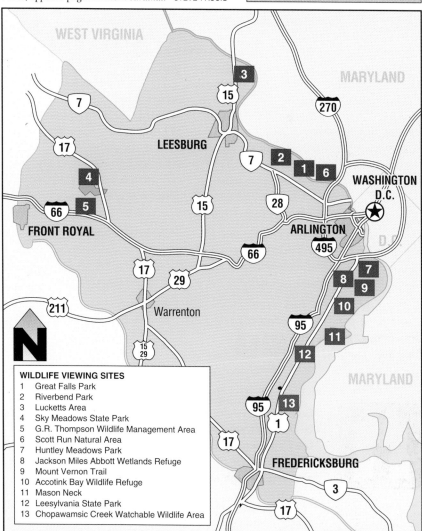

WILDLIFE VIEWING SITES
1 Great Falls Park
2 Riverbend Park
3 Lucketts Area
4 Sky Meadows State Park
5 G.R. Thompson Wildlife Management Area
6 Scott Run Natural Area
7 Huntley Meadows Park
8 Jackson Miles Abbott Wetlands Refuge
9 Mount Vernon Trail
10 Accotink Bay Wildlife Refuge
11 Mason Neck
12 Leesylvania State Park
13 Chopawamsic Creek Watchable Wildlife Area

21

1 GREAT FALLS PARK

Description: Forcing its way through a narrow gorge and series of imposing rock outcroppings, the Potomac River plunges in a dramatic series of waterfalls and cascades at Great Falls Park. Appreciated for striking scenery and some of the best viewing of migrating songbirds in Northern Virginia, Great Falls encompasses oak-hickory woodlands, hardwood swamp, young second-growth forest, and open, park-like habitats.

Viewing Information: Six hiking trails permit wildlife viewers to access most regions of the park. During spring, chances are excellent for viewing a number of warblers, including the yellow-rumped, northern parula, black-and-white, Kentucky, and American redstart. Many songbirds nest at Great Falls such as the eastern wood pewee, great crested flycatcher, Carolina chickadee, tufted titmouse, white-breasted nuthatch, Carolina wren, and wood thrush. During summer along the Potomac, look for great blue and green-backed heron, and in the river look for mallard and wood duck. During the fall, migrating warblers, purple finches, and cedar waxwings can be viewed, while winter brings such waterfowl as the common merganser, bufflehead, common goldeneye, ring-necked duck, mallard, and black duck. Four species of woodpecker inhabit the park year round: red-bellied, downy, hairy, and the pileated, Virginia's largest woodpecker. Virginia's state bird, the cardinal, is a year-round resident. Overall, about 150 species of birds can be seen here at one time of the year or another. In the woodlands along the Ridge Trail, Old Carriage Road Trail, and Matildaville Trail, look for white-tailed deer and gray squirrel. In the park's more open areas, cottontail rabbits can be seen. In these same areas, there is a chance of catching a glimpse of a gray fox, since cottontails are an important food source for gray fox.

Directions: At the junction of Interstate 495 (northwest of Washington, D.C.) and VA PR 193 (Georgetown Pike), follow VA PR 193 west approximately 4.2 miles to VA SR 738 (Old Dominion Drive). Turn right and follow VA SR 738 approximately 1 mile to the park entrance.

Ownership: National Park Service (703) 285-2966
Size: 800 acres   **Closest Town:** Great Falls

Much of the excitement of wildlife viewing stems from the fact that you can never be sure of what you will see. Many species are difficult to see even under the best of circumstances. Wildlife viewing requires patience; spending enough time in the field is critical.

2 RIVERBEND PARK

Description: Two miles upriver from Great Falls, Riverbend Park offers diverse habitats, 12 miles of trails, a visitor center, nature center, bird blinds, and excellent interpretive guides.

Viewing Information: The Potomac River directly in front of the visitor center is excellent for viewing waterfowl, especially 2 major duck groups: dabbling, or puddle ducks such as mallard, pintail, wood duck, and black duck; and diving ducks including bufflehead and common merganser. Dabbling ducks feed by tipping underwater for grasses and plant seeds. They take flight directly from the water. Diving ducks submerge underwater to eat small fish, crustaceans, mollusks and aquatic plants. They must "patter" along the water to gain speed before taking flight. Look for bald eagles near the river's aqueduct dam or perched in snags (standing dead trees). Reach the dam via the blue-blazed Potomac Heritage Trail to the south; to the trail's north, look for wild turkey around the pond nearest the Potomac. Chances are excellent for seeing deer and songbirds, including the Carolina chickadee, tufted titmouse, white-breasted nuthatch, and Carolina wren along the red-blazed upland trail. White-tailed deer and cottontail rabbits are usually seen around trails across Jeffery Road from the nature center. Walk the white-blazed *duff 'n stuff* trail and the pawpaw passage trail in summer to observe tiger swallowtail or zebra swallowtail butterflies. Zebra swallowtail caterpillars feed exclusively on pawpaw. *ENTRANCE FEE DURING SUMMER WEEKENDS FOR FAIRFAX COUNTY NONRESIDENTS. COLLECTING WITHIN THE PARK IS PROHIBITED.*

Directions: *West of Washington, D.C, take Interstate 495 to VA PR 193 (Georgetown Pike), follow VA PR 193 west approximately 4.5 miles to VA SR 603 (Riverbend Road). Go right (north) on VA SR 603 to VA SR 1268 (Jeffery Road). Go right (east) on Jeffery Road and follow to park entrance.*

Ownership: Fairfax County Park Authority (703) 759-3211
Size: 409 acres   **Closest Town**: Great Falls

Eastern tiger swallowtail.
BARBARA GERLACH

3 LUCKETTS AREA

Description: Open farming country, scattered woodlots, small streams, and ponds characterize Lucketts' rural, privately-owned farmland. A long-time favorite among Northern Virginia and Washington birders, Lucketts area also hosts a number of mammal, reptile, and amphibian species.

Viewing Information: Many gravel roads transect from U.S. 15, offering unhurried viewing opportunities. VA SR 657, 658, 661, and 662 amble through open areas where white-tailed deer can be seen in the early morning and late afternoon. Watch for red-tailed hawks and kestrels flying overhead, perched in trees, or on power lines in fields. Between March and September, eastern bluebirds perch on roadside fences and near the many bluebird nesting boxes constructed throughout the area. Look for cottontail rabbits in fields and keep attentive for red fox along the edge of the woodlots. Listen for bobwhite calling across fields or scurrying for cover. *PRIVATE PROPERTY. PLEASE VIEW FROM ROADS; DO NOT TRESPASS.*

Directions: *From Leesburg, take U.S. Highway 15 north to VA SR 661, 657, 662, or 658. The Lucketts Area is to the right (east) of U.S. 15.*

Ownership: Privately owned   **Closest Town:** Leesburg

4 SKY MEADOWS STATE PARK

Description: Sky Meadows State Park offers wildlife viewers a remarkable blend of American history, natural history, and some of the most beautiful scenery in the entire Commonwealth. The park now encompasses parcels of land owned at one time by Lord Fairfax, George Washington, Revolutionary War Captain John Edmonds, and George Slater, one of John Mosby's first Rangers. Habitats include pastures, streams, springs, ponds, and upland forest.

Viewing Information: Excellent songbird viewing. In the early morning, look for year-round residents Carolina chickadee, tufted titmouse, northern mockingbird; eastern wood-pewee can be seen in summer. In the less densely-wooded areas, look for such woodpeckers as the red-bellied, red-headed, and downy. Gray and fox squirrels may be seen in the woodlands. Look for white-tailed deer at dawn and dusk along the forest edge. *CAMPING IS PRIMITIVE AND HIKE-IN ONLY.*

Directions: *From Interstate 66, take U.S. Highway 17 north approximately 6 miles; the park is on the left.*

Ownership: Virginia Department of Conservation and Recreation (703) 592-3556 **Size:** 1,900 acres   **Closest Town:** Paris

5 | G.R. THOMPSON WILDLIFE MANAGEMENT AREA

Description: Located on the eastern slope of the Blue Ridge Mountains, this site is best known among wildlife enthusiasts for its spectacular spring wildflower display and abundant viewing opportunities of migrating hawks in the fall. A mature mixed hardwood forest is the most common habitat type while the most notable are spring seeps.

Viewing Information: The remarkably showy large-flowered trillium display can be viewed at the highest elevations along VA SR 638 in May. The best way to view the flower show, however, is to hike along the Appalachian Trail (A.T.) which bisects the wildlife management area. The A.T. can be reached from Parking Areas 4 and 7 and access points along VA SR 638. From Parking Area 4, the A.T. is 0.75 mile down the blue-blazed Ted Lake Trail (old road); from Parking Area 7, a gated old road leads to the trail, which is about 0.25 mile from the parking area. September through November, migrating sharp-shinned, rough-legged, red-tailed, red-shouldered, and broad-winged hawks can be seen from the A.T. near the openings at the firetower along VA SR 638, and near Parking Area 14, which is about 3 miles north of Parking Area 7. *NATURAL AREA WITH NO FACILITIES. PUBLIC HUNTING AREA: PLEASE CHECK WITH MANAGER FOR AFFECTED AREAS AND SEASONS.*

Directions: From Front Royal, take Interstate 66 east to Linden or Markham exits. VA SR 638 north from Linden borders the west edge of the site and VA SR 688 north from Markham borders the east edge of the site.

Ownership: Virginia Department of Game and Inland Fisheries (703) 899-4169; or contact Appalachian Trail Conference (304) 535-6331.
Size: 4,500 acres   **Closest Town:** Front Royal

The large-flowered trillium can easily be identified by its large, solitary white flower and yellow anthers.
WILLIAM B. FOLSOM

Description: Scott Run Natural Area, formerly Dranesville District Park, offers wildlife viewers and wildflower enthusiasts serene landscapes and quiet respite only minutes from Washington's busy Capital Beltway. Several habitats exist within the area, including oak-hickory forest, floodplains, steep slopes/palisades, fields, thickets, and an eastern hemlock stand, unusual this far east. The area also boasts 175 species of wildflowers and a 12-foot-high waterfall along Scott Run.

Viewing Information: While hiking 12 trails in the natural area, viewing probability is high for white-tailed deer, squirrel, cottontail rabbit, and songbirds such as the white-breasted nuthatch, tufted titmouse, Carolina chickadee, and Carolina wren. *NATURAL AREA WITH NO FACILITIES. GEORGETOWN PIKE IS A VERY BUSY ROAD; PLEASE USE CAUTION WHEN ENTERING OR EXITING THE PARKING AREAS.*

Directions: *At the junction of Interstate 495 and VA PR 193 (Georgetown Pike) northwest of Washington, D.C., follow VA PR 193 west approximately 0.25 mile to a small parking lot on the right or 0.5 mile to the main parking lot, also on the right.*

Ownership: Fairfax County Park Authority (703) 759-3211
Size: 336 acres   **Closest Town:** McLean

Description: Only 10 miles from the U. S. Capitol, Huntley Meadows Park is a wildlife sanctuary amidst Northern Virginia's sprawling cities and suburbs. Extensive beaver activity has produced emergent, shrub, and forested wetlands abundant in wildlife. Young and mature upland forests surround grass-shrub meadow, which offer more wildlife diversity. Excellent interpretive facilities include a visitor center, 4-mile hike-bike trail, and a 2-mile, self-guided interpretive trail system with a boardwalk and wildlife viewing platforms.

Viewing Information: In the early morning and late afternoon, beaver, muskrat, and river otter might be seen in the wetland. Take the boardwalk to view wading birds such as the great blue, green-backed, and yellow-crowned night heron; American bittern; and king and Virginia rail. On spring evenings in the meadows off the hike-bike trail, woodcocks zigzag and dart about overhead. The park's upland habitats sustain owls, white-tailed deer, fox, and a host of songbirds.

Directions: *Take U.S. Highway 1 about 3.5 miles south from the Capital Beltway. Turn right onto Lockheed Boulevard and travel 0.5 mile to park entrance on left.*

Ownership: Fairfax County Park Authority (703) 768-2525
Size: 1,261 acres   **Closest Town:** Alexandria

8 | JACKSON MILES ABBOTT WETLANDS REFUGE

Description: Dedicated to Lieutenant Colonel Jackson Miles Abbott for his significant contributions to wildlife conservation, this refuge within Fort Belvoir contains a freshwater pond and wetlands.

Viewing Information: From the parking lot, follow the trail 0.1 mile to a trail turning right. From there, walk another 0.1 mile to Mulligan Pond. The trail around the pond leads to a freshwater wetlands area. Look for beaver and muskrat, or signs of their presence, in and around the stream, marsh, and pond. Although these semi-aquatic mammals are nocturnal, they are occasionally seen during daylight. Beavers can be easily distinguished from muskrats by their larger size and flattened, paddle-shaped tail; a muskrat's tail, by comparison, is narrow and ropelike. Adult beavers weigh between 30 and 60 pounds, while adult muskrats weigh between 2 and 4 pounds. Look for beaver dams and dens: large piles of sticks, twigs, mud, and even small logs across the stream, or large conical mounds of sticks and mud at the water's edge. Muskrats build smaller, dome-shaped houses of herbaceous plants in marshes, or dens in stream and pond banks. Viewing a bald eagle flying overhead is especially rewarding here, considering that Colonel Abbott's 30-year survey of bald eagles played a critical role in identifying the detrimental effects of the pesticide DDT. *NATURAL AREA WITH NO FACILITIES.*

Directions: From Interstate 95 in Fairfax County, take the Newington/Fort Belvoir exit. Turn south onto Backlick Road toward Fort Belvoir, travel approximately 4 miles. Turn left onto U.S. Highway 1 (north), travel to Old Mill Road next to Woodlawn Plantation, and turn left. Follow Old Mill Road to Pole Road (VA SR 622), turn right. Refuge entrance is 0.2 mile on left.

Ownership: U.S. Department of the Army (703) 806-4007
Size: 146 acres   **Closest Town:** Alexandria

A muskrat's tail is compressed laterally, and its hairless, ropelike appearance distinguishes this semi-aquatic mammal from any other. LEONARD LEE RUE III

Description: This seventeen-mile hiking, biking, historical and wildlife-watching trail meanders from Arlington Memorial Bridge to Mount Vernon, George Washington's estate and burial place. Running parallel to the Potomac River, the trail passes through deciduous forest and along tidal freshwater marshes and large mudflats. The trail also passes through or near Hunting Creek Bay, Fort Hunt Park, Jones Point Park, and Dyke Marsh, where over 250 species of birds have been observed.

Viewing Information: Dabbling ducks such as black duck, mallard, and others appear along the river throughout the year. Between November and March, diving ducks such as lesser scaup, ruddy duck, and canvasback are found on the Potomac. Common loons are often seen along the river. During April and May, and between July and September, sandpipers and terns are found along the mudflats: look for the spotted, solitary, semipalmated, least, pectoral, and white-rumped sandpiper, as well as the Caspian and Forster's tern; semipalmated plover is also seen here during these times. On the mudflats during spring and summer, look for killdeer. Great blue heron, Canada goose, and red-tailed hawk are present year-round. Four species of gull (laughing, ring-billed, herring, and great black-backed) fly near the river, where viewing chances are excellent. Bald eagles sometimes soar over George Washington's Mount Vernon, due to an eagle nest on the grounds.

Directions: Between Mount Vernon and the Arlington Memorial Bridge, the George Washington Memorial Parkway runs along the trail for much of its length. It can be accessed from the Lyndon Baines Johnson Memorial Grove, Belle Haven, Mount Vernon, and several other overlooks.

Ownership: National Park Service (703) 285-2598
Size: Trail approximately 17 miles long **Closest Town:** Alexandria, Arlington

Common tern. JOHN GERLACH

10 ACCOTINK BAY WILDLIFE REFUGE

Description: Located at the mouth of Accotink Creek, this refuge contains diverse habitats, including tidal marsh, wetlands, streams, beaver ponds, bottomland hardwood forests, hardwood forested slopes, and upland deciduous forests. Nine hiking trails traverse the refuge, including 2 self-guided interpretive trails. A newly-constructed boardwalk into the marsh and a barrier-free trail enhance viewing opportunities of 243 bird species, 22 mammal species, and scores of fish, reptiles, and amphibians that inhabit Fort Belvoir.

Viewing Information: The wide variety of habitats supports an array of wildlife. A beaver lodge can be seen in the marsh along Beaver Pond Trail—look for gnawed stumps and the characteristic pile of sticks, logs, and mud of a beaver den. Listen for the characteristic "slap" of water as a beaver dives below the surface; the sound is made by the tail striking the water and warns others in the colony of potential danger. There is a good probability of seeing a bald eagle over Accotink Bay, especially during winter. Walk the Great Blue Heron Trail during the spring and look for wading birds, including great blue and green-backed heron, in and around the marsh. Hike the Cemetery Loop Trail during most times of the year and look for waterfowl such as mallard, wood duck, and black duck in the marshes. Five different species of woodpecker are found in the refuge throughout the year: the red-bellied, downy, and hairy woodpecker, along with the northern flicker, which is common, and the less common pileated woodpecker, which is the largest species. Migrating waterfowl use the refuge but aren't the only wildlife that migrate through the refuge; gizzard shad also pass through as they move upstream to spawn.

Directions: From Interstate 95 in Fairfax County, take the Newington/Fort Belvoir exit. Turn south onto Backlick Road towards Fort Belvoir and travel about 4 miles to U.S. Highway 1. Go through the light at U.S. 1 onto Pohick Road (Backlick Road turns into Pohick Road after crossing U.S. 1). Enter Fort Belvoir through Tulley Gate on Pohick Road and travel 0.75 mile; the refuge is on the right.

Ownership: U.S. Department of the Army (703) 806-4007
Size: More than 1,300 acres   **Closest Town:** Alexandria

One of the greatest challenges while wildlife watching is positively identifying the animals you see. Many animals have distinctive "field marks" that distinguish one species from another. Learn these field marks and wildlife identification becomes easier and more accurate.

11 MASON NECK

Description: Mason Neck is an 8,000-acre peninsula on the shores of the Potomac River, named after the Mason family and the homesite of George Mason, father of the Bill of Rights. Viewing sites at Mason Neck consist of Mason Neck National Wildlife Refuge and Mason Neck State Park. The national wildlife refuge was established specifically to protect critical nesting, feeding, and roosting habitat for bald eagles. The state park, located directly west of the refuge on Belmont and Occoquon Bay, is also a haven for bald eagles and hundreds of other wildlife species.

Viewing Information: In the refuge, Great Marsh Trail offers spectacular views of 258-acre Great Marsh. Chances of seeing the majestic bald eagle at Great Marsh are good. During winter, 50 to 60 eagles occur along the peninsula (fewer than 20 are present in summer). Look for the distinctive white head and white tail of adult eagles. Although young bald eagles lack the white head and tail, they can still be identified by their size and flight; immature bald eagles might be confused with golden eagles, which are actually quite rare at Mason Neck. When suspecting a bird at a considerable distance to be a bald eagle, observe the way it flies. Bald eagles soar flat-winged, as opposed to the characteristic "V" wingspread of turkey vultures. In the state park during winter, look for eagles above Bay View Trail and Kane's Creek Trail. Although the bald eagle is the star at Mason Neck, there is also a distinguished supporting cast. The refuge contains a rookery with over 1,200 PAIRS of great blue herons. Three-mile-long Woodmarsh Trail offers views of Great Marsh where beaver, muskrats, marsh hawks, wading birds, and migrating waterfowl can be seen. This trail leads to an observation deck overlooking a beaver dam. Over 200 species of birds have been identified at Mason Neck. The peninsula is also excellent for viewing reptiles and amphibians.

Directions: From junction of U.S. Highway 1 and VA PR 242 (Gunston Hall Road) in Fairfax County, travel east on VA PR 242 about 5 miles. At Mason Neck Wildlife Refuge, bear right and follow High Point Road about 3 miles to Mason Neck State Park entrance.

Ownership: State Park managed by Virginia Dept. of Conservation and Recreation, (703) 550-0960; refuge managed by U.S. Fish & Wildlife Service, (703) 690-1297.

Size: State Park 1,804 acres; Refuge 2,227 acres   **Closest Town**: Lorton

Plumage on the head and tail of the bald eagle does not become white until the bird reaches four or five years of age.

12 LEESYLVANIA STATE PARK

Description: A National Historic Landmark, Leesylvania was home to Henry Lee II, father of Revolutionary War hero Light-Horse Harry Lee and Grandfather of Confederate General Robert E. Lee.

Viewing Information: Waterfowl, including the mallard, black duck, wood duck, canvasback, bufflehead, and merganser, are seen in winter and spring. Two eagle nests near the park increase the possibility of seeing one overhead. Eagles roost along Bushey Point and Freestone Point throughout the winter. Osprey can be seen over the river in spring and summer, while tundra swans are observed in winter along Powell's Creek. Early mornings and evenings, look for white-tailed deer along the nature or historic trail.

Directions: From junction of U.S. Highway 1 and Neabsco Road (between Woodbridge and Dumfries), travel east on Neabsco Road for approximately 1 mile to park entrance on right.

Ownership: Virginia Department of Conservation and Recreation (703) 670-0372

Size: 508 acres
Closest Town: Woodbridge

13 CHOPAWAMSIC CREEK WATCHABLE WILDLIFE AREA

Description: The U.S. Marine Corps has constructed a viewing platform and wildlife trail (North Bank Trail) to offer easy access to Chopawamsic Creek and surrounding freshwater tidal wetlands.

Viewing Information: From fall to late winter in mornings and late afternoons, the observation platform offers excellent viewing of dabbling ducks such as mallard, pintail, black duck, wood duck, and American wigeon; tundra swan and Canada goose are also present. A bald eagle nest and a great blue heron rookery located on Quantico Marine Corps Base increase chances of viewing these birds between mid-April and mid-July. During the herring run in late April and early May, observe osprey diving for these fish. *A DRIVER'S LICENSE IS NECESSARY TO ENTER BASE. HUNTING BLINDS ARE WITHIN SIGHT OF THE WILDLIFE VIEWING PLATFORM, BUT ARE WELL OUT OF GUNSHOT RANGE; THERE IS NO SAFETY HAZARD.*

Directions: From Interstate 95, take Exit 148, Quantico Marine Corps Base (south of Triangle). Travel east on Russell Road about 2 miles to a sentry station. Obtain a visitor pass and proceed 2 miles. Turn right at the wildlife viewing area sign.

Ownership: United States Marine Corps (703) 640-5810
Size: 400 acres   **Closest Town:** Quantico

REGION TWO: EASTERN SHORE

Geographically and psychologically, Virginia's Eastern Shore is a world apart. Bound by barrier islands and the Atlantic Ocean on the east, and the Chesapeake Bay, the largest estuary in North America, on the west, Virginia's 70 miles of Eastern Shore is a wildlife watcher's haven. The great diversity of habitats support numerous wildlife species. These wildlife habitats include ocean, sandy beach, dunes, pine and oak forests, and salt and fresh water marshes. Located along the Atlantic flyway, the region boasts spectacular displays of migrating birds, especially in the fall.

Photo, opposite page: snow geeese. BILL LEA

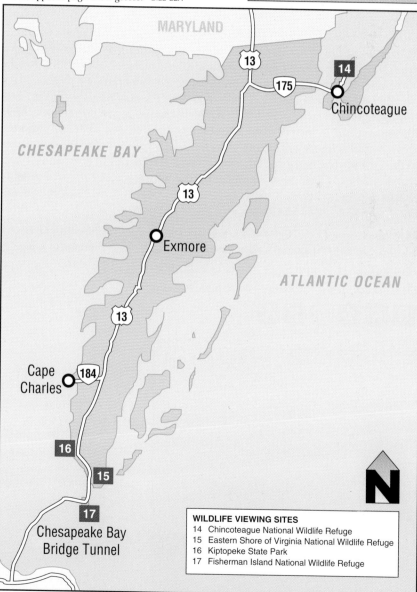

WILDLIFE VIEWING SITES
14 Chincoteague National Wildlife Refuge
15 Eastern Shore of Virginia National Wildlife Refuge
16 Kiptopeke State Park
17 Fisherman Island National Wildlife Refuge

Description: Considered one of the nation's premiere wildlife viewing locales, Chincoteague, Indian for "beautiful land across the waters," offers much to explore. The refuge is part of a larger complex of public land preserved to protect the area's rich biological diversity, including the Assateague Island National Seashore and Assateague State Park.

Viewing Information: Chincoteague and Assateague Island's diverse habitats and strategic location along the Atlantic flyway host a wide variety of species. Each season offers different viewing opportunities as many of the birds to be viewed here are migratory. Perhaps the most spectacular viewing occurs at aptly-named Snow Goose Pool between October and March, where hundreds of snow geese can be observed; mute and tundra swans may also be seen at this time. During summer along many miles of undeveloped shore, look for the bottlenose dolphin, sanderling, semipalmated sandpiper, brown pelican, black skimmer, and several species of gull, including the laughing, ring-billed, herring, and greater black-backed. Pine warblers can be seen in pine forests, while the endangered Delmarva fox squirrel might be observed in heavily-wooded areas. Between September 15 and October 15, this area is one of the best places in the U.S. to view peregrine falcons. Overall, 316 species of birds and 44 species of mammals have been identified on the refuge, making it a true wildlife watcher's paradise. *PUBLIC HUNTING AREA: CONTACT MANAGER FOR AFFECTED AREAS AND SEASONS.*

Directions: From U.S. Highway 13, take VA PR 175 east to Chincoteague Island. Go north on Main Street, turn right onto Maddox Boulevard; continue to refuge.

Ownership: U. S. Fish and Wildlife Service (804) 336-6122
Size: 13,700 acres   **Closest Town:** Chincoteague

Chincoteague's wetlands offer numerous wildlife viewing opportunities. Feeding here are snow geese, Canada geese, and the famous Chincoteague wild ponies.
GARY A. HUMPHREY

15 EASTERN SHORE OF VIRGINIA NATIONAL WILDLIFE REFUGE

Description: Salt marsh, beach dunes, maritime forest, grasslands, freshwater ponds and wetlands, and myrtle and bayberry thickets characterize this refuge located on the southernmost tip on the Delmarva Peninsula. This is an important staging ground for migrating birds before they cross the 18-mile expanse of open water over the mouth of the Chesapeake Bay.

Viewing Information: Situated at the tip of the cone-shaped Delmarva Peninsula, migrating fall birds are literally "funneled" into the refuge, where fabulous opportunities to view migrating songbirds and hawks abound between September and November. During these months there is a high probability of observing the American kestrel, merlin, sharp-shinned hawk, tree swallow, eastern bluebird, and many different warblers, including yellow-rumped, pine, and yellow. There is an elevated wildlife viewing platform on the 0.75-mile wildlife trail, located just south of the refuge headquarters, where most species of raptors can be viewed readily during fall migration. Viewers can look for the eastern box turtle during spring and summer after rain showers along this trail, and in summer test their butterfly identification skills as they differentiate monarchs, swallowtails, and sulphurs. At the Visitor Center Pond there is a good chance of viewing the glossy ibis, snowy and great egret, and green-backed heron in the summer; mallard and greater and lesser yellowlegs may be viewed there during the spring. *PUBLIC HUNTING AREA: CONTACT MANAGER FOR AFFECTED AREAS AND SEASONS.*

Directions: *From Cape Charles, take U.S. Highway 13 south for 10 miles, turn left onto Seaside Road (last exit before the Bay Bridge-Tunnel), travel 0.25 mile to refuge entrance.*

Ownership: U.S. Fish and Wildlife Service (804) 331-2760
Size: 651 acres   **Closest Town:** Cape Charles

American kestrels are often seen perched on snags and transmission lines along roads. The wings of adult males are blue-gray, while females are rusty-brown.

ROB & MELISSA SIMPSON

35

Description: The Commonwealth's only state park on the Eastern Shore, Kiptopeke is located directly on the Chesapeake Bay and offers spectacular open-water vistas, coastal dunes, open fields, and upland mixed forests. There are well-developed beaches because of sunken ship breakers off shore, as well as boardwalks, trails, and a fishing pier open 24 hours a day.

Viewing Information: Kiptopeke is known nationwide for its spectacular viewing opportunities of raptors and songbirds during fall migration, and since 1963 it features extensive bird banding, as well as the Kiptopeke Raptor Research site. Ornithologists have estimated that upwards of 15,000 raptors, mostly sharp-shinned hawks, pass through the area each fall. From the fishing pier or the beach in the morning and late afternoon during winter, there is a good chance of viewing several diving duck species, including bufflehead, American goldeneye, canvasback, red-breasted merganser, oldsquaw, surf scoter, and white-winged scoter. Summer offers excellent opportunities to see Atlantic bottlenose dolphin, brown pelican, and several species of gull, sandpiper, and tern.

Directions: From Cape Charles, take U.S. Highway 13 south to VA SR 704 (about 7 miles). Go west on to VA SR 704 Kiptopeke Drive; travel 0.25 mile to the entrance of the park.

Ownership: Virginia Department of Conservation and Recreation (804) 331-1040
Size: 375 acres
Closest Town: Cape Charles

Boardwalks at Kiptopeke State Park offer excellent wildlife viewing locales for people while protecting fragile habitat for wildlife. SUSAN M. GLASCOCK

Description: Accessible only through refuge-sponsored guided-tours, this 1,000-acre refuge is located on a barrier island at the mouth of the Chesapeake Bay. Situated one half-mile south of the southern tip of the Delmarva Peninsula, the island is the last land stop before miles of open water over the mouth of the Chesapeake Bay. As a result, migrating birds stage (gather in large groups) at the refuge, waiting for appropriate weather conditions to cross the bay.

Viewing Information: Informative 2- to 4-hour guided tours allow visitors to get the most out of their visit. Literally millions of passerines such as eastern bluebirds, eastern meadowlarks, and tree swallows stage on the island during fall migration, where there is a high probability of viewing hundreds at any one time. Migrating raptors, including the sharp-shinned, Cooper's, and red-tailed hawk, also stage on the island. Peregrine falcons can be seen on the hacking tower. Guided tours are available on Saturdays, October to March; October and November are best for seeing migrating songbirds and raptors. Make reservations well in advance by calling the refuge office. There are no facilities on the island.

Directions: The refuge is an island located at the north end of the Chesapeake Bay Bridge Tunnel on U.S. Highway 13, 0.5 mile south of the Delmarva Peninsula. Access is through guided tours only through the Eastern Shore of Virginia National Wildlife Refuge.

Ownership: U. S. Fish and Wildlife Service (804) 331-2760 or 331-3425
Size: 1,000 acres
Closest Town: Cape Charles

Thousands of sharp-shinned hawks pass through the Eastern Shore each fall during migration.
BARBARA GERLACH

REGION THREE: TIDEWATER

River, bay, and ocean converge in the tidewater region, as 4 major rivers—the Potomac, Rappahanock, York, and James—flow into the Chesapeake Bay, and ultimately, the Atlantic Ocean. Rising gradually from the Bay and Atlantic Ocean, the coastal plain here is divided into 3 major peninsulas. From north to south, these are commonly referred to as the "northern neck," "middle peninsula," and "the peninsula." As the oldest settled region of America, it is fitting that the area is one of the best sections in the Commonwealth to view the bald eagle, national symbol of the United States.

Photo, opposite page: great blue heron.   JOHN GERLACH

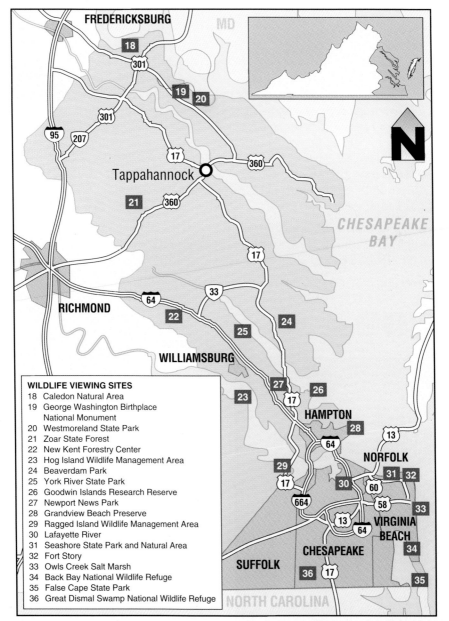

WILDLIFE VIEWING SITES
18 Caledon Natural Area
19 George Washington Birthplace
    National Monument
20 Westmoreland State Park
21 Zoar State Forest
22 New Kent Forestry Center
23 Hog Island Wildlife Management Area
24 Beaverdam Park
25 York River State Park
26 Goodwin Islands Research Reserve
27 Newport News Park
28 Grandview Beach Preserve
29 Ragged Island Wildlife Management Area
30 Lafayette River
31 Seashore State Park and Natural Area
32 Fort Story
33 Owls Creek Salt Marsh
34 Back Bay National Wildlife Refuge
35 False Cape State Park
36 Great Dismal Swamp National Wildlife Refuge

Description: Named after Caledonia, the majestic forest of Scotland, the Caledon area is summer home to one of the largest bald eagle concentrations in the east. Five miles of hiking trails, guided eagle watching tours, and an interpretive center concentrating on bald eagles and their natural history provide a spectrum of information and opportunities to view eagles.

Viewing Information: Bald eagles occur between mid-June and September 1 with good viewing probability. Guided tours, available from mid-June until Labor Day, are the best way to visit. Wildlife viewers also can hike trails unguided; all 5 trails are open year-round. Look for eagles flying overhead or over the Potomac River or marsh. Bald eagles fly with flattened wings, unlike vultures that soar with their wings in a "V" and ospreys that fly with "bent" wings. Identify eagles at a distance by their great size and wingspan of 7 to 8 feet. Mature birds have characteristic white heads and tails; immature birds are dark. While flying overhead, immature eagles show some white underneath their wings. Primarily fish-eaters, eagles swoop down and use sharp talons to seize fish from the marsh and Potomac; they will also harass ospreys to steal their freshly- caught fish. *PLEASE CALL FOR RESERVATIONS FOR GUIDED TOURS. BALD EAGLE PROTECTION ZONES ARE CLOSED TO THE PUBLIC; PLEASE RESPECT THESE AREAS. TRAILS ARE FOR HIKING ONLY; MOTORIZED VEHICLES AND BICYCLES ARE PROHIBITED.*

Directions: *From Fredericksburg, take VA PR 218 east 19 miles to viewing area; or from U.S. Highway 301 in King George County, take VA PR 206 west 4 miles to VA PR 218, then go west about 1 mile to viewing area.*

Ownership: Virginia Department of Conservation and Recreation (703) 663-3861
Size: 2,579 acres   **Closest Town:** King George

The wingspan of a bald eagle is 7 to 8 feet. Bald eagles feed primarily on fish, but also feed on waterfowl, rabbits, muskrats, and squirrels.
LYNN M. STONE

19 GEORGE WASHINGTON BIRTHPLACE NATIONAL MONUMENT

Description: George Washington was born at Popes Creek Plantation on February 22, 1732. Located on a peninsula bordered by the Potomac River and Popes Creek, the monument's several habitats provide homes for many species.

Viewing Information: Between December and February, large flocks of tundra swans can be seen in Popes Creek. Swans may also be seen in the Potomac River. Bald eagles are readily seen on Popes Creek near the information center. Between October and February, look for canvasbacks and large flocks of Canada geese. Waterfowl are found on the water; geese use the cornfields.

Directions: From Fredericksburg, take VA PR 3 to VA PR 204 in Westmoreland County, travel east on VA PR 204 about 2 miles to monument.

Ownership: National Park Service (804) 224-1732
Size: 538 acres **Closest Town:** Colonial Beach

20 WESTMORELAND STATE PARK

Description: High on the cliffs of the Potomac River, Westmoreland offers dramatic, panoramic water views. Six miles of hiking trails lead wildlife viewers through dense hardwood forests and profuse thickets of mountain laurel.

Viewing Information: Chances are excellent of seeing white-tailed deer early mornings or late afternoons throughout the year. In early mornings or evenings look for wild turkey in grassy clearings. There are good chances of viewing eagles overhead or perched in snags along the Potomac. Viewers may catch glimpses of river otter, muskrat, or beaver along the park's waterways. Near the water during spring, listen for the calls of green treefrogs (a "queenk"), southern leopard frogs (a series of "croaks" followed by 2 or 3 "clucks"), and bullfrogs, the largest in Virginia ("jug-o'-rum"). Search for fossilized shark teeth in the lower beach area after high water or rainstorms. *DIGGING FOSSILS IS ILLEGAL WITHOUT PERMISSION, BUT SHARK TEETH FOUND MAY BE LEGALLY KEPT.*

Directions: From Montross, take VA PR 3 west about 4 miles to park entrance on right. Or, from Fredericksburg, take VA PR 3 east to park entrance on left (about 40 miles).

Ownership: Virginia Department of Conservation and Recreation (804) 493-8821
Size: 1,300 acres **Closest Town:** Montross

21 ZOAR STATE FOREST

Description: Upland and bottomland hardwood dominate this small state forest on the Mattaponi River in King William County. Begin to explore on Zoar Nature Trail, a 1-mile self-guided footpath.

Viewing Information: Zoar Nature Trail begins on an upland bluff, meanders through exquisite bottomland hardwood forests along the Mattaponi River, and returns viewers to the bluff. There is a good chance of viewing yellow-bellied sapsucker in winter, or its signs: rows of small holes encircling live trees. The trail's upland portion provides excellent viewing opportunities for white-tailed deer, wild turkey, and gray squirrel. Great blue heron, beaver, and wood duck inhabit the river and wetlands. *NATURAL AREA WITH NO FACILITIES.*

Directions: Take U.S. Highway 360 west from Tappahannock. Cross over the Mattaponi River and turn right onto VA SR 600 (west) in Aylett. Travel west 1.5 miles to trail entrance on right.

Ownership: Virginia Department of Forestry (804) 977-6555
Size: 378 acres   **Closest Town:** Aylett

22 NEW KENT FORESTRY CENTER

Description: Initially established to produce tree seedlings and implement a tree improvement program, the center encompasses seedbeds, orchards, open fields, hardwood forests, cypress stands, and marshlands. To date, the center has produced over 65 million loblolly pine seedlings, and boasts an award-winning nature trail. Its admirable environmental education materials are designed to cover several of the Virginia Department of Education's Standards of Learning.

Viewing Information: Hike the New Kent Nature Trail on the western end of the center's grounds. View deer, wild turkey, and gray squirrel year-round from over 600 feet of boardwalk with viewing platforms. The 1-mile, one-way trail leads through a bald cypress swamp to the Chickahominy River. At the river, look for several species of waterfowl and wading birds such as great blue heron.

Directions: From Providence Forge in New Kent County, take U.S.Highway 60 east 3 miles to Forestry Center on right.

Ownership: Virginia Department of Forestry (804) 966-2201
Size: 850 acres   **Closest Town:** New Kent

Description: Not an island at all, but a peninsula jutting out into the brackish waters of the James River, this site combines loblolly pine stands, large cultivated fields, shallow freshwater impoundments, tidal marshlands, and riverine habitats. Dirt roads, a viewing tower, and a large network of primitive trails allow access to numerous viewing locales and sweeping views of fields, marshes, and the James River.

Viewing Information: Winter at Hog Island is hog heaven for wildlife watchers. In mornings and evenings, Canada geese graze by the thousands on fields of wheat and grain planted for them. Observe hundreds of diving ducks: the hooded merganser, common merganser, and ring-necked duck; and puddle ducks: the American wigeon, northern pintail, and green-winged teal. Many tundra swan can be seen as well. Spring brings the horned lark, blue-winged teal, spotted sandpiper, solitary sandpiper, glossy ibis, and water pipit. The fulvous whistling duck and glossy ibis are rare, but might be seen. View bald eagle with good probability in summer, and in fall the multitude of ducks returns. View shorebirds, great and snowy egret, and several species of heron (great blue and green-backed) with high probability. Chances of seeing mourning dove, quail, wild turkey, and white-tailed deer are good near food patches planted for upland species. *PUBLIC HUNTING AREA: PLEASE CHECK WITH MANAGER FOR AFFECTED AREAS AND SEASONS.*

Directions: From Williamsburg, travel west on VA PR 31 (Jamestown Road) to Surry, crossing the James River via the Scotland-Jamestown Ferry. Turn left onto VA PR 10, continue east for about 8 miles to Bacon's Castle. Turn left (east) onto VA SR 617, drive about 1 mile, then turn left (north) onto VA SR 650. Travel north about 5 miles to viewing area.

Ownership: Virginia Department of Game and Inland Fisheries (804) 367-1000
Size: 3,900 acres   **Closest Town:** Williamsburg

TIDEWATER

Although male and female Canada geese are visually similar, their calls are distinct. Listen carefully for the low "a-honk" of the male and the higher "hink" of the female.
LYNDA RICHARDSON

43

24 BEAVERDAM PARK

Description: Gloucester County constructed this 635-acre reservoir in 1990 to provide drinking water for residents. A self-guided, 3-mile nature trail with 4 separate loops borders the lake's northeast end.

Viewing Information: View several beaver lodges in the back end of the lake's several coves by boat or from the nature trail's orange-blazed fourth loop. Look for beaver activity late in the afternoon during summer; listen for the loud warning "slap" caused by its tail. During late fall and winter, look for bald eagles perched in snags across the lake. Osprey fly over the lake in summer in search of a meal.

Directions: From Gloucester Court House, travel north on U.S. Business 17 for 0.25 mile to VA SR 616; turn right and travel northeast on VA SR 616 (Roaring Springs Road) to parking area.

Ownership: Gloucester County (804) 693-2107

Size: 635 acres   **Closest Town:** Gloucester Court House

25 YORK RIVER STATE PARK

Description: Freshwater and saltwater converge where the 2-mile-wide York River flows toward the Chesapeake Bay, creating critical estuarine wildlife habitats. Fifteen miles of trails span freshwater and saltwater wetlands, mixed hardwood forests, and over 3 miles of riverfront. A self-guided nature trail passes through the brilliant green saltmarsh of Taskinas Creek, a component of the Chesapeake Bay National Estuarine Research Reserve in Virginia.

Viewing Information: Frequent sightings of woodland mammals include white-tailed deer, fox, and raccoon, as well as sightings of bald eagle, osprey, and great blue heron. Many birds rarely seen elsewhere on the coastal plain inhabit this park. From the observation deck in summer, look for the yellow-throated vireo and worm-eating warbler; during migration, see solitary vireo, hermit and wood thrush, yellow-billed cuckoo, and various warbler species: chestnut-sided, blackburnian, Canada, black-throated blue, and green. The ruby-crowned and golden-crowned kinglet appear in winter, when many duck species are present. Find belted kingfisher and river otter near Taskinas Creek.

Directions: From Interstate 64 (west of Williamsburg), take VA SR 607 (Croaker Road) at exit 231B; travel 0.5 mile north on VA SR 607 to VA SR 606 (Riverview Road), turn right. Continue 2 miles east on VA SR 606 to park entrance on left.

Ownership: Virginia Department of Conservation and Recreation (804) 566-3036
Size: 2,505 acres
Closest Town: Williamsburg

Description: Located on the south side of the mouth of the York River, this pristine viewing site is an archipelago of saltmarsh islands *ACCESSIBLE BY BOAT ONLY.* A component of the Chesapeake Bay National Estuarine Research Reserve in Virginia, the islands are surrounded by submerged aquatic vegetation beds, oyster reefs, and shallow estuarine waters; they contain saltmarsh, maritime scrub, bottomland pine forest, mixed hardwood uplands, seagrass meadows, mudflats, and beaches.

Viewing Information: The quality of wildlife viewing and near-pristine nature of the islands more than counter the obstacle of reaching this site. Shallow draught boats in the islands' channels provide excellent views of marsh species. Two more ways to view wildlife are walking the beaches to see shore and water species, and hiking the network of upland trails on the western end of the main island to view migratory birds in the fall. View great blue heron year-round in the marshes. Many species of waterfowl are present in winter — ruddy duck, oldsquaw, bufflehead, red-breasted merganser, scoter, and common goldeneye. There is a large heron rookery on the eastern half of the main island. During spring and fall migration, several species of sandpiper can be seen: solitary, spotted, western, semipalmated, and least; also view dunlin, dowitcher, yellowlegs, and ruddy turnstone. Other shorebirds include the semipalmated and black-bellied plover, and killdeer. Sandpipers are best seen at low tide on beaches and flats along the eastern islands and main channel. View the clapper rail on mornings with an ebbing tide. Least terns are common in late summer. In summer, see loggerhead turtles in open water around seagrass beds; diamondback terrapins on sunny days at the cove on the eastern side of the eastern islands; and fiddler, blue, and hermit crab in the marshes and shallows. *ORGANIZED GROUP TOURS TO THE ISLAND ARE PERIODICALLY CONDUCTED BY THE VIRGINIA LIVING MUSEUM AT (804) 595-1900. ORGANIZED VOLUNTEER WILDLIFE MONITORING ACTIVITIES ARE CONDUCTED PERIODICALLY BY THE CHESAPEAKE BAY NATIONAL ESTUARINE RESEARCH RESERVE IN VIRGINIA AT (804) 642-7135. NATURAL AREA WITH NO FACILITIES.*

Directions: The islands are east of Yorktown at the mouth of the York River. The reserve can be accessed by boat only. Public ramps at Back Creek, Gloucester Point, and Jenkins Neck provide 10-20 minute access. Identification signs surround the reserve.

Ownership: Chesapeake Bay National Estuarine Research Reserve in Virginia, College of William and Mary (804) 642-7135

Size: More than 1,600 acres   **Closest Town:** Yorktown

TIDEWATER

45

27 NEWPORT NEWS PARK

Description: This extensive park is located only a few miles northwest of the congestion and bustle of the Norfolk - Newport News metropolis. The park contains a 360-acre lake, a 5.3-mile bikeway, and over 30 miles of hiking trails through mixed hardwood forests, marsh, and shore habitats.

Viewing Information: The 2.6-mile White Oak Nature Trail is an excellent place to view gray squirrel, white-tailed deer, raccoon, songbirds, pileated woodpecker, and, in winter, yellow-bellied sapsucker. The prothonotary warbler can usually be seen in spring and summer from the swamp boardwalk.

Directions: From Newport News, take Interstate 64 west to exit 250B, Jefferson Avenue (VA PR 143). Turn left on VA PR 143 and travel north, past Fort Eustis Boulevard (VA PR 105), to park entrance on right.

Ownership: Newport News (804) 888-3333
Size: More than 8,000 acres
Closest Town: Newport News

28 GRANDVIEW BEACH PRESERVE

Description: Extensive salt marsh, coastal thicket (predominantly wax myrtle), and undeveloped Chesapeake Bay beaches characterize this preserve, accessed only by foot.

Viewing Information: From the parking lot, the trail leads to the beach, which runs north for about 2 miles to the peninsula's end, jutting into the Chesapeake Bay. During summer, observe the laughing gull, tern species (royal, Forster's, common, least), and brown pelican along the beach. Fall and spring bring dunlin, sanderling, red knot, and ruddy turnstone. Look for marsh wren, Virginia and clapper rail, heron, egret, least bittern, seaside sparrow, and common yellowthroat in the marshes, where swallowtail butterflies (zebra, tiger, and eastern black) may also be seen. In winter, see common goldeneye, red-breasted merganser, oldsquaw, and horned grebe on the water. Viewers find white-tailed deer year-round. *A LEAST TERN NESTING COLONY IS AT THE PENINSULA'S FAR END; PLEASE RESPECT MARKED BOUNDARIES; NATURAL AREA WITH NO FACILITIES.*

Directions: At junction of Interstate 64 and U.S. Highway 258 in Hampton, travel east on U.S. 258 about 3 miles to VA PR 169 (Fox Hill Road). Follow Fox Hill Road north to the beach, following signs to Grandview.

Ownership: City of Hampton Department of Parks (804) 727-6347
Size: 578 acres   **Closest Town:** Hampton

29 RAGGED ISLAND WILDLIFE MANAGEMENT AREA

Description: Situated along the south side of the James River in Isle of Wight County, this management area contains boardwalks and platforms to view excellent examples of tidal, salt marsh, and pine hammock habitats.

Viewing Information: The best viewing is from the boardwalk, accessed at the parking area across the bridge on the left-hand side of the road. Fall and winter provide excellent opportunities to view diving ducks such as canvasback, scaup, and redhead in the river. View bald eagle, white-tailed deer, and gray squirrel year-round. *NATURAL AREA WITH NO FACILITIES. PUBLIC HUNTING AREA: PLEASE CHECK WITH MANAGER FOR AFFECTED AREAS AND SEASONS.*

Directions: *From Newport News, take U.S. 17 south across James River Bridge. Site is immediately south of the bridge.*

Ownership: Virginia Department of Game and Inland Fisheries (804) 253-7072
Size: 1,537 acres
Closest Town: Newport News

30 LAFAYETTE RIVER

Description: Tanner's Creek, as the Lafayette River was known from Colonial days to World War II, has been described as "a wildlife oasis amidst expansive metropolitan sprawl." It flows directly through Virginia's largest metropolitan area. Though engulfed by the City of Norfolk, the urban river remains relatively healthy and maintains exceptional wildlife diversity.

Viewing Information: Best seen by canoe or rowboat, the river has 2 launching spots near the Granby Street Bridge. In summer, look for brown pelican, cormorant, kingfisher, tern species, and black skimmer along the river. As many as 600 pairs of yellow-crowned night herons are easily seen in the summer along marsh edges from a boat. Fall brings diving ducks like bufflehead and canvasback. Winter is excellent for viewing merganser and grebe, while spring is best for great blue heron and egret. *NATURAL AREA WITH NO FACILITIES.*

Directions: *The river lies on the western side of Norfolk. At junction of Interstate 64 and U.S. Highway 460, follow U.S. 460 (Granby Street) south to the river. After crossing the bridge, either turn after 0.25 mile right on Delaware Ave. and go 2 blocks, or turn after 0.5 mile left on Lavallette Ave. and launch at the end of the street.*

Ownership: City of Norfolk
Size: 5-mile section of river   **Closest Town:** Norfolk

TIDEWATER

Description: The Commonwealth's most-visited state park, Seashore contains a multitude of watchable wildlife. Almost 20 miles of hiking trails amble through bald cypress swamps, salt marsh, dunes, and maritime forest.

Viewing Information: Begin a trip to Seashore by stopping at the visitor center to pick up the series of checklists for park ferns, trees, birds, wildflowers, reptiles and amphibians, and mammals. Walk the 1.5-mile self-guided Bald Cypress Trail, replete with observation decks and boardwalks; look for great blue heron, green-backed heron, snowy egret, gray treefrog, green frog, spring peeper, pileated woodpecker, hairy and downy woodpecker, and several turtle species, including the redbelly, yellowbelly slider, and the endangered chicken turtle. In the evening here, raccoons might be seen along the marsh feeding on fish, mice, snails, and insects. Fox Run Trail, considered one of the best birding trails, is a good place to view the parula and prothonotary warbler in summer, when osprey nest along Long Creek Trail. At the end of White Hill Trail, look for fiddler crabs. Two species of rabbit can sometimes be seen in late afternoon — the eastern cottontail, and marsh. Marsh rabbits are generally browner than cottontails and lack the prominent white tail. Over 150 birds, almost 20 mammals, and almost 50 reptiles and amphibians have been recorded here.

Directions: In Virginia Beach, travel west on U.S. Highway 60 (Atlantic Avenue) to park entrance.

Ownership: Virginia Department of Conservation and Recreation (804) 481-2131 or (804) 481-4836

Size: 2,892 acres   **Closest Town:** Virginia Beach

The bald cypress swamps at Seashore State Park are home to a variety of reptiles, amphibians, birds, and mammals. Seashore is the only known location in Virginia that supports the endangered chicken turtle. SUSAN M. GLASCOCK

Description: Fort Story is a military reservation situated on Cape Henry, on the south side of the mouth of the Chesapeake Bay. On April 26, 1607, America's first permanent English settlers (the Jamestown colonists) made their first New World landfall here.

Viewing Information: Atlantic bottlenose dolphin can be viewed from the First Landing Cross Observation Deck (Cape Henry Overlook). This overlook provides an observation deck for wildlife viewing and panoramic water views. Small groups of dolphin are best seen swimming parallel to the shore during early morning or late evening from April to mid-November when the water is relatively calm. Fort Story is one of the best spots to see the little gull, usually mixed in with larger flocks of Bonaparte's gull in the fall. *A VALID DRIVER'S LICENSE IS NECESSARY TO ENTER THE RESERVATION.*

Directions: *At junction of U.S. Highway 60 and U.S. 13 in Virginia Beach, travel east on U.S. 60 and follow signs to the reservation.*

Ownership: U.S. Department of Defense (804) 422-7305
Size: 1,450 acres   **Closest Town:** Virginia Beach

TIDEWATER

Atlantic bottlenose dolphin are often seen swimming along the shore at Fort Story.
ANJA BURNS

Description: The only remaining salt marsh connected directly to the ocean in Virginia Beach, Owls Creek has the highest salinity of any Virginia mainland marsh. The site's elevated interpretive boardwalk behind the Virginia Marine Science Museum offers several outstanding educational stations. The U.S. Navy designated the forested area across the creek a watchable wildlife area, the Navy's first in the Commonwealth.

Viewing Information: During spring through fall, look for great blue heron and great egret in the creek's marsh or shallows, and fiddler crab at low tide below the boardwalk. Fiddler crabs blend into the marsh and at first appear to be insects as they quickly scurry across the mud. During spring and summer in the freshwater pond, look for bullfrogs and freshwater turtles. The museum sponsors summer dolphin watch boat trips and winter whale watch boat trips; call for information and reservations.

Directions: In Virginia Beach, take U.S. 60 east and cross the Rudee Inlet Bridge. Virginia Marine Science Museum is located approximately 0.5 mile on the right.

Ownership: Virginia Marine Science Museum (804) 437-4949
Size: 13.75 acres   **Closest Town:** Virginia Beach

Hundreds of fiddler crabs are present beneath the boardwalk at Owls Creek Salt Marsh. JOHN SHAW

Description: One of Virginia's premiere wildlife viewing locales. Ocean, beach, sand dunes, shrublands, maritime forest, marsh, and bay habitat typify this vital barrier island refuge. Intensive wildlife management activities such as water level manipulation, prescribed burning, dike construction, disking, and seasonal closures of vital habitat enhance wildlife abundance.

Viewing Information: Viewing is exclusively by foot via the beach, trails, and boardwalk. December's viewing is spectacular, when up to 10,000 snow geese use the refuge; look for snow and Canada geese on Back Bay and the impoundment pools. Large flocks of feeding gannets can be seen just off the beach in fall and winter. Between October and March in open, shallow pools, look for waterfowl; observe northern harrier with its distinctive white rump gliding over the marsh or pools. In spring, see various migrating songbirds and shorebirds. In summer in the marshes, look for many different wading birds; green-backed heron may be seen in the canals, along with turtles and river otter. View glossy and white ibis in the pools, and gulls, terns, and pelicans on the beach where ghost crabs scurry around. Watch the ocean for bottlenose dolphins. On higher elevations (shrub and woodlands) look for white-tailed deer, gray squirrel, and marsh rabbit. Fall brings migratory waterfowl; look for peregrine falcon along the beach. *PLEASE CHECK WITH MANAGER FOR SEASONAL CLOSURES. MOTOR VEHICLES ARE ALLOWED ONLY ON THE ENTRANCE ROAD AND PARKING AREA.*

Directions: *At junction of VA PR 44 (Virginia Beach Toll Road) and Birdneck Road in Virginia Beach, travel south about 2 miles on Birdneck Road to General Booth Boulevard. Travel south (right) about 4 miles on General Booth Blvd. to Princess Anne Rd., go south (left) on Princess Anne less than 0.5 mile to Sandbridge Road. Follow Sandbridge Road east about 4.5 miles to Sandpiper Road. Go right (south) on Sandpiper Road which leads to the refuge after approximately 4.5 miles.*

Ownership: U. S. Fish and Wildlife Service (804) 721-2412
Size: 7,700 acres
Closest Town: Virginia Beach

TIDEWATER

The only sea turtle that nests in Virginia, the Atlantic loggerhead can weigh in excess of 350 pounds as an adult. Here tiny loggerhead hatchlings scurry for the surf at Back Bay. Biologists estimate that only one in several thousand hatchlings reach adulthood.

LYNDA RICHARDSON

35 FALSE CAPE STATE PARK

Description: Situated on Virginia's southeast corner, the park is bordered on the north by Back Bay National Wildlife Refuge, and by the state of North Carolina on the south. Hiking, biking, and boating are the only modes of transportation into this park, managed as a pristine and undeveloped barrier spit. Explore over 7 miles of hiking trails, including 2 interpretive trails, 2 viewing towers, 4 primitive camping sites, and an environmental education center.

Viewing Information: The overlook on Barbour Hill Interpretive Trail (north end) is best for viewing white-tailed deer and waterfowl. Wash Woods Interpretive Trail (park's middle to south portion) contains interpretive signs and an observation tower. Look for deer, raptors, and gray fox at dawn and dusk. In the marsh, find river otter and red-winged blackbird, sanderling, and gulls. In the Atlantic, bottlenose dolphin are found in summer, and winter and early spring sometimes show humpback whale. Atlantic right whale and finback whale are present in winter, though chances of seeing these mammals are slight. Excellent viewing of peregrine falcon in fall. *ACCESS THROUGH BACK BAY NATIONAL WILDLIFE REFUGE BY FOOT OR BICYCLE ONLY. BRING WATER. PARK CLOSED FIRST FULL WEEK IN OCTOBER FOR CONTROLLED MANAGEMENT HUNT.*

Directions: At junction of VA PR 44 (Virginia Beach Toll Road) and Birdneck Road in Virginia Beach, travel south about 2 miles on Birdneck Road to General Booth Boulevard. Travel right (south) about 4 miles on General Booth Blvd. to Princess Anne Rd., go left (south) on Princess Anne Road less than 0.5 mile to Sandbridge Road. Follow Sandbridge Road east about 4.5 miles to Sandpiper Road. Go right (south) on Sandpiper Road which leads to Back Bay National Wildlife Refuge after approximately 4.5 miles. Follow trails south through the refuge to the park.

Ownership: Virginia Department of Conservation and Recreation (804) 426-7128
Size: 4,300 acres
Closest Town: Virginia Beach

Whale watching is an increasingly popular activity in Virginia. Organizations such as the Virginia Marine Science Museum now sponsor winter whale watch boat trips, where wildlife watchers may get a glimpse of a whale like this humpback.
FREDERICK D. ATWOOD

Description: The Great Dismal Swamp ecosystem has been drastically changed during the past 2 centuries by repeated logging, drainage, farming, and commercial and residential development. The refuge is now a mosaic of forested wetlands, a remnant marsh, a sphagnum bog, an evergreen shrub community, 3,100-acre Lake Drummond, a natural lake, and a series of drainage ditches from times past.

Viewing Information: The main public use area is located at the Washington Ditch entrance. The Washington Ditch road provides access to Lake Drummond. Also located here is the Boardwalk Trail, a 0.75-mile trail through the swamp. Almost 210 species of birds come through the refuge, 93 of which nest there. The peak for birding at the swamp is between April and May. Chances of seeing common yellowthroat and blue-winged, Swainson's, prothonotary, and Wayne's black-throated green warbler are good in early mornings and late afternoons. In winter, snow geese and tundra swan are viewed on Lake Drummond. Many mammals exist in the refuge: otter, beaver, muskrat, mink, raccoon, gray and red fox, gray squirrel, white-tailed deer, eastern cottontail and marsh rabbit, black bear, and bobcat. From spring to fall, view almost 80 reptile and amphibian species. Yellow-bellied, spotted, and eastern painted turtle are seen in the ditches; bullfrog and spring peeper live in and around small ponds. Three species of poisonous snakes inhabit the refuge: eastern cottonmouth or water moccasin, canebrake rattlesnake (a variation of the timber rattlesnake), and northern copperhead. *PUBLIC HUNTING AREA: PLEASE CHECK WITH MANAGER FOR AFFECTED AREAS. REFUGE CLOSED DUSK TO DAWN.*

Directions: *From Suffolk, take U.S. Highway 13 south to VA PR 32. Travel south on VA PR 32 for 4.5 miles and follow signs to refuge.*

Ownership: U. S. Fish and Wildlife Service (804) 986-3705
Size: 82,150 acres
Closest Town: Suffolk

TIDEWATER

Marsh rabbits occur in Virginia only in the southeastern portion of the Commonwealth. This species ranges from southeastern Virginia to Florida.
LYNDA RICHARDSON

REGION FOUR: CENTRAL

Gently rising from the coastal plain on the east to the blue ridge on the west, the Central Virginia region is piedmont country. Dominated by oak - pine forests, several large bodies of water distinguish the region. The Commonwealth's largest inland body of water, John Kerr Reservoir, is found here. This reservoir is 50,000 acres and has 800 miles of shoreline; to the west, 20,000 acre Smith Mountain Lake has 500 miles of shoreline. The extensive shoreline of these and the many other lakes of Central Virginia are attractive habitats for both wildlife and people.

Photo, opposite page: zebra swallowtail.

JOHN NETHERTON

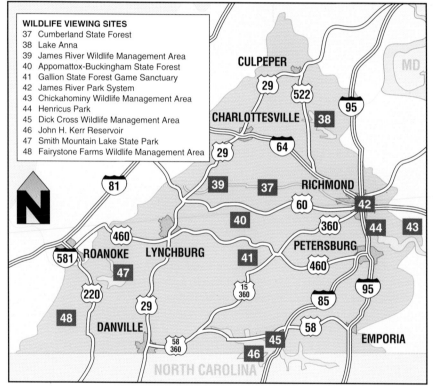

WILDLIFE VIEWING SITES
37 Cumberland State Forest
38 Lake Anna
39 James River Wildlife Management Area
40 Appomattox-Buckingham State Forest
41 Gallion State Forest Game Sanctuary
42 James River Park System
43 Chickahominy Wildlife Management Area
44 Henricus Park
45 Dick Cross Wildlife Management Area
46 John H. Kerr Reservoir
47 Smith Mountain Lake State Park
48 Fairystone Farms Wildlife Management Area

CENTRAL

55

37 CUMBERLAND STATE FOREST

Description: With such varied habitats as lakes, rivers, bottomland hardwood forests, upland hardwood forests, and fields and streams, the many sites within Cumberland State Forest offer wildlife viewers numerous and varied viewing opportunities.

Viewing Information: There are several viewing sites within the forest. The state forest surrounds Bear Creek Lake State Park, an excellent locale to view wood duck, great blue heron, many species of songbirds and abundant spring wildflowers, such as pink lady's slipper and jack-in-the-pulpit. The forest contains 4 small, picturesque lakes. The surrounding hardwood forest and shores of Winston Lake offers exceptional opportunities to view white-tailed deer, wild turkey, gray squirrel, great blue heron, and muskrat. A foot trail around the lake offers easy access. The forest also contains 4 natural areas — Willis River, Rock Quarry, Red Cedar, and Turkey Ridge. Willis River Natural Area, remote but accessible, encompasses 38 acres of bottomland hardwood forest on an alluvial floodplain. A swinging bridge provides a gateway to the Willis River Trail, where beaver, muskrat, deer, wild turkey, and wood duck can be observed; the swinging bridge provides a chance to view bass, northern pike, and bluegill in the river. *PUBLIC HUNTING AREA: PLEASE CHECK WITH MANAGER FOR AFFECTED AREAS.*

Directions: TO BEAR CREEK LAKE STATE PARK: From Cumberland (between Richmond and Lynchburg), take U.S. Highway 60 east to VA SR 622 on left (Trents Mill Road). Go 4 miles on VA SR 622 and make a left onto VA SR 629. Follow to park entrance. TO CUMBERLAND STATE FOREST: Follow directions to Bear Creek Lake State Park and follow signs to forest. WINSTON LAKE is located on the left continuing on VA SR 629. WILLIS RIVER NATURAL AREA: At junction of U.S. 60 and VA PR 45, take VA PR 45 north 6.5 miles to VA SR 663 on left (Game Farm Road). Follow Game Farm Road and continue on Game Farm Road turning left on VA SR 615 (Game Farm Road). Follow VA SR 615 for 2 miles to VA SR 608 (Sugar Fork Road) and take a right. Follow VA SR 608 for less than 1 mile and make a right onto Warner Forest Road and follow until the road ends at the swinging bridge. The head of the trail starts after the swinging bridge. PUBLIC HUNTING AREA: PLEASE CHECK WITH MANAGER FOR AFFECTED AREAS.

Ownership: Virginia Department of Conservation and Recreation (804) 492-4121
Size: 16,500 acres
Closest Town: Cumberland

Night vision goggles open up a previously unseen night world and greatly enhance viewing such animals as bats, owls, raccoons, and bears.

38 LAKE ANNA

Description: Widely-varied habitats surrounding many-armed Lake Anna, such as pine and deciduous forests, open farming country, marshes, and shoreline, support hundreds of wildlife species.

Viewing Information: The Big Woods Trail behind the state park visitor center is a good place to start exploring Lake Anna. From spring to fall, look for beaver and the beaver lodge while hiking the trail. Beaver may also be seen along Railroad Ford Trail. In the marshes look for muskrat, great blue heron, and red-winged blackbird. Many songbirds, waterfowl, hawks, common loon, and belted kingfisher are present at various times around the lake.

Directions: Take Interstate 95 south of Fredericksburg to Thornburg. At I-95 and VA SR 606 junction (Thornburg), take VA SR 606 west for approximately 4 miles. At Snell, VA SR 606 joins VA PR 208. Follow VA PR 208 west for approximately 11 miles. Turn right onto VA SR 601 and travel 4 miles. Turn left onto VA SR 7000 and follow to park entrance.

Ownership: Virginia Department of Conservation and Recreation (703) 854-5503
Size: 2,058 acres   **Closest Town:** Bells Cross Road

39 JAMES RIVER WILDLIFE MANAGEMENT AREA

Description: Pine and oak-hickory dominate hilly woodlands that slope to flatlands. Intensive wildlife management efforts such as food plantings, nest boxes, and water manipulation enhance wildlife numbers and diversity.

Viewing Information: During fall and winter in early mornings or evenings on the ponds, marsh, and river, look for wood duck, mallard, black duck, northern pintail, and blue-winged teal. Canada geese and 10 species of salamander are present. Hike the gated trails to see white-tailed deer, wild turkey, bobwhite, and such songbirds as eastern bluebird and cardinal. In the wetlands near the ponds and marsh, look and listen for bullfrog and pickerel frog. Beaver and river otter live in the James River. *PUBLIC HUNTING AREA: PLEASE CHECK WITH MANAGER FOR AFFECTED AREAS.*

Directions: From Lovingston, take VA PR 56 south 14 miles to VA SR 626 (Howardsville Road). Turn left and follow for less than 1 mile. Turn right onto VA SR 743. Follow signs to the marsh project or to the boat launching ramp.

Ownership: Virginia Department of Game and Inland Fisheries (804) 432-1377
Size: 1,312 acres   **Closest Town:** Wingina

40 ▌ APPOMATTOX-BUCKINGHAM STATE FOREST

Description: There are many exceptional viewing sites to explore here. The state forest envelops Holliday Lake State Park, which offers a 113-acre lake and 3 hiking trails through wetlands and pine, cedar, and hardwood forests.

Viewing Information: North of Holliday Lake State Park lies Holiday Creek Natural Area. This is a 37-acre area dominated by upland hardwoods and shortleaf pine forests. The upland hardwood section is located at the southeastern section of the intersection of VA SR 614 and 692, while the Virginia pine forest is located slightly southeast of the upland hardwood section. Hike the gated trail which passes through both. White-tailed deer, wild turkey, raccoon, gray squirrel, and eastern chipmunk are present. Exquisite displays of pink lady's slipper can be viewed in the spring. *NATURAL AREA WITH NO FACILITIES. PUBLIC HUNTING AREA: PLEASE CHECK WITH MANAGER FOR AFFECTED AREAS.*

Directions: *To Holliday Creek Natural Area, from Appomattox (east of Lynchburg), take VA PR 24 east for 6 miles to Vera. At junction of VA PR 24 and VA SR 616, turn right to follow VA SR 616 to VA SR 614. Turn left and follow VA SR 614 to VA SR 618, turn left on VA SR 618 and then a right back onto VA SR 614. Follow VA SR 614 to VA SR 692 and turn right onto VA SR 692 and go to parking area on left.*

Ownership: Virginia Department of Forestry (804) 983-2175
Size: 19,705 acres   **Closest Town:** Appomattox

41 ▌ GALLION STATE FOREST GAME SANCTUARY

Description: The rolling Piedmont of hardwood forests, pine plantations, and open fields support many upland species. The Gallion Forest Road winds through this sanctuary, displaying gracious views of the countryside.

Viewing Information: White-tailed deer, wild turkey, gray squirrel, cottontail rabbit, and bobwhite are present, as are both gray and red fox. Look for deer during the early morning and late afternoon in forest clearings. *NATURAL AREA WITH NO FACILITIES. THERE IS NO HUNTING WITHIN THE SANCTUARY BUT THERE IS HUNTING IN OTHER SECTIONS OF THIS FOREST: PLEASE CHECK WITH MANAGER FOR AFFECTED AREAS.*

Directions: *At junction of U.S. Highway 360 and VA SR 696 at Green Bay, take VA SR 696 north to the forest. Turn left onto Gallion Forest Road which leads through the sanctuary.*

Ownership: Virginia Department of Forestry (804) 983-2175
Size: Approximately 400 acres   **Closest Town:** Green Bay

42 JAMES RIVER PARK SYSTEM

Description: By canoe, kayak, or foot, the falls of the James River and the James River Park System are considered the best wildlife viewing locales in the Richmond area. Boasting striking scenery, the James River flows swiftly through Virginia's capital city, dropping over 100 feet in 7 miles, creating a mixture of whitewater, deep pools, and flatwater. This park system consists of 6 areas along the river. From west to east these are Huguenot Woods, Pony Pasture/Wetlands, Main Section, North Bank, Belle Isle, and Ancarrow's Landing. The falls comprise a section of the river which is a Virginia Scenic River. Many canoeists and kayakers consider this stretch of the James River to have the best urban whitewater in the United States.

Viewing Information: On and near the river during summer, look for great blue heron, green-backed heron, osprey, wood duck, Canada goose, cormorant, muskrat, and river otter. During fall, look for bald eagle overhead or perched in trees along the river. Winter brings bufflehead to the river. Spring mornings are an excellent time to view warblers; over 20 species might be seen, such as the black-and-white, northern parula, yellow, yellow-rumped, and prairie. Snorkeling is another popular way to observe aquatic life below the water. Pick up the Department of Recreation's guide, "Snorkeling in the City: Underwater Exploration of the James River in Richmond" for further information. Snorkelers have a chance of seeing American freshwater mussel, several species of river snail, crayfish, and many species of fish, such as the bull chub, mosquitofish, satinfin shiner, sunfish, smallmouth bass, and longnose gar. Aquatic diversity is high in this section of the James; it is the interface between tidal and nontidal waters and resident fish mix with migrant species. *PLEASE USE EXTREME CAUTION WHILE NEAR AND ON THE RIVER.*

Directions: The James River Park System runs along Riverside Drive in Richmond on the south side of the river. There are units of the park system along the north side of the James as well. Start out at the Information and Comfort Station at Reedy Creek in the Main Section on the south side of the river off of Riverside Drive and Hillcrest Road (near 42nd Street).

Ownership: City of Richmond, Department of Recreation and Parks (804) 780-5311
Size: More than 400 acres
Closest Town: Richmond

CENTRAL

Wildlife is often closer and more abundant than many people think. While looking for wildlife, work on heightening your senses of sight and sound. Look for subtle movements in bushes, shrubs, and trees. Move slowly and quietly. Slowing down and being quiet greatly enhances the chances of seeing wildlife.

Description: Located on the peninsula between the York and James rivers on the Chickahominy River, 12 miles northwest of Williamsburg, this management area encompasses tidal creeks, tidal brackish marsh, mixed upland hardwood and pine stands, and riverine habitats.

Viewing Information: The boat ramp at Morris Creek provides access for viewing many species at various times of the year along the marshes, creek, and river: great blue heron, wood duck, and black duck are present year-round. Listen for ruffed grouse drumming in spring. Pied-billed grebe can be seen in the winter. During summer, look for beaver and muskrat in the marshes. Bald eagle and osprey might be seen in the summer; some eagles are present year-round. Several parking areas throughout the management area provide stopping places to get out and hike. Walk along the management area roads or trails to see upland species such as wild turkey, gray squirrel, cottontail rabbit, and mourning dove. White-tailed deer are present throughout the management area. The red-bellied woodpecker, downy woodpecker, northern flicker, and pileated woodpecker nest in the area. *NATURAL AREA WITH NO FACILITIES. PUBLIC HUNTING AREA: PLEASE CHECK WITH MANAGER FOR AFFECTED AREAS.*

Directions: *At junction of VA SR 614 and VA SR 615, turn left (east) onto VA SR 615, follow for 4 miles. At junction of VA SR 615 and VA SR 623 turn right (south) onto VA SR 623, follow for about 1 mile to VA SR 621. Turn left and follow to viewing site.*

Ownership: Virginia Department of Game and Inland Fisheries (804) 829-5336
Size: 6,200 acres   **Closest Town**: Providence Forge

Barred owls are more likely to be heard than seen. Listen for the distinctive loud hooting at night: "hoohoo-hoohoo, hoohoo-hoohooaw."

JOHN GERLACH

44 HENRICUS PARK

Description: Henricus Park is the site of the second English settlement in Virginia, dating to 1611. There are numerous wildlife observation locales along the trail leading to the historical site.

Viewing Information: Access to the park is by foot. The 1.5-mile historical trail winds through riparian woodlands leading to a grassy area and bluff overlooking the James River. The park contains a heron rookery. White-tailed deer and beaver are present. Look for pileated woodpecker in wooded areas flying from tree to tree. Red-shouldered hawk, barred owl, and prothonotary warbler nest in the park. Bald eagle might be seen in winter.

Directions: From Chester south of Richmond, take VA PR 10 east about 0.25 mile past Interstate 95 to Old Stage Road. Turn left to travel north on Old Stage Road for 2 miles, make a right onto access road immediately before the Virginia Power Chesterfield Power Station and follow to the Dutch Gap boat ramp parking area. The trailhead is at the far end of the parking lot.

Ownership: Chesterfield County Parks and Recreation (804) 748-1623
Size: 32 acres
Closest Town: Chester

45 DICK CROSS WILDLIFE MANAGEMENT AREA

Description: Large old fields, marsh, cultivated fields, shallow water impoundments, and intensive wildlife management efforts attract a wide diversity of wildlife to Dick Cross Wildlife Management Area, formerly Elm Hill Wildlife Management Area.

Viewing Information: Shallow impoundments, the Roanoke River, and a beaver swamp provide excellent viewing of waterfowl and shorebirds in winter. Bald eagles are also present at this time of year along the river. In summer, look for bobwhite and wild turkey in the early morning or late afternoon in and near clearings. Red-tailed and red-shouldered hawk are year-round residents. Look for red-shouldered hawk in the lower, wetter areas of the management area, where they feed mostly on snakes and frogs. Look for red-tailed hawk in the drier uplands; they feed mostly on small rodents. *NATURAL AREA WITH NO FACILITIES. PUBLIC HUNTING AREA: PLEASE CHECK WITH MANAGER FOR AFFECTED AREAS.*

Directions: From U.S. Highway 58 in Mecklenberg County, go south on VA PR 4 about 4 miles to management area entrance on left.

Ownership: Virginia Department of Game and Inland Fisheries (804) 367-1000
Size: 1,400 acres   **Closest Town:** Boydton

Description: Eight hundred miles of mostly wooded shoreline encircle this reservoir, Virginia's largest inland body of water. The U. S. Army Corps of Engineers manages 24 wildlife management areas scattered around the reservoir. Occoneechee State Park contains 2,700 acres on the northwestern shore. (Also, see site 45).

Viewing Information: Begin with the "Guide to Wildlife Management Areas," available at the Corps of Engineers' Visitor Center-Resource Management Center located 0.5 mile southwest of the dam on VA SR 678. The waters below the dam on winter early mornings offer some of the best bald eagle viewing in the Commonwealth. During winter, the reservoir is one of the best inland viewing areas for waterfowl: look for the black duck, gadwall, green-winged and blue-winged teal, American wigeon, shoveler, redhead, ring-necked duck, canvasback, lesser scaup, common goldeneye, bufflehead, ruddy duck, hooded merganser, common merganser, and red-breasted merganser. The common and red-throated loon are also present at this time in the lake's lower reaches. Cliff swallows nest on the dam in spring after migrating north from South America. Many wading birds are seen along the shores year-round, including green-backed heron and great blue heron. In spring and fall, see great and snowy egret along lake edges and in marshes. White-tailed deer, gray squirrel, cottontail rabbit, opossum, and red and gray fox inhabit the forests and open areas around the lake. Many wildlife management areas have no facilities. Occoneechee State Park offers camping and other amenities. *MANY SURROUNDING LOCATIONS ARE PUBLIC HUNTING AREAS: PLEASE CHECK WITH MANAGERS FOR AFFECTED AREAS.*

Directions: From Boydton in Mecklenberg County, go east on U.S. Highway 58 for 6 miles to VA PR 4. Take VA PR 4 south to the dam.

Ownership: U.S. Army Corps of Engineers (804) 738-6143
Size: 50,000 acres
Closest Town: Boydton

The poisonous copperhead occurs throughout the Commonwealth. Note the characteristic dark-brown "hourglass" pattern running down the snake's back.
ADAM JONES

47 ■ SMITH MOUNTAIN LAKE STATE PARK

Description: Enjoy panoramic views of 20,000-acre Smith Mountain Lake in Virginia's rolling Piedmont country. Five hundred miles of shoreline provide endless opportunities for exploration and wildlife observation.

Viewing Information: Although wildlife such as white-tailed deer can be viewed while slowly driving in the park, the best way to savor Smith Mountain's biodiversity is to hike one of the park's many trails. Hike the green-blazed Turtle Island Trail or the red-blazed Chestnut Ridge Trail for panoramic water views. Songbird viewing is excellent throughout the park. Near the forest edges in the morning near the campground, look for bobwhite and wild turkey. In the early evening in open areas near lights during summer, look for the eastern pipistrelle bat erratically flying around. Spring wildflowers, such as bluets and sweet white violets, are impressive and abundant.

Directions: From Bedford, east of Roanoke, take VA PR 122 south for 13 miles to VA SR 608. Turn left and travel east to VA SR 626, then turn right (south) onto VA SR 626 and follow to park entrance.

Ownership: Virginia Department of Conservation and Recreation (703) 297-6066
Size: 1,506 acres
Closest Town: Huddleston

48 ■ FAIRYSTONE FARMS WILDLIFE MANAGEMENT AREA

Description: Dominated by mixed oaks, hickories, and white pine on steep upland soils, with poplar, beech, and rhododendron along the narrow valleys, the area provides habitat for white-tailed deer, wild turkey, gray squirrel, and a variety of other species. Fairystones are small crystals composed of iron aluminum silicate and shaped like roman and St. Andrew's crosses. According to legend, when fairies learned the tragic news of Christ's crucifixion they wept crystallized tears, the fairy stones found in the vicinity.

Viewing Information: Waterfowl viewing is good along the Smith River and Philpott Reservoir borders. Look for dabbling ducks in late evenings and early mornings during spring and fall. Several parking areas along VA SR 822 provide access to foot trails into the area. *NATURAL AREA WITH NO FACILITIES. PUBLIC HUNTING AREA: PLEASE CHECK WITH MANAGER FOR AFFECTED AREAS.*

Directions: From Bassett, take VA PR 57 west for 7 miles to VA SR 822. Turn right and drive to Goose Point Road. Or continue on VA PR 57 past VA SR 822 and turn right onto VA PR 346, then left on VA SR 623, then left at first gravel road to Adams Tract and Marsh projects.

Ownership: Virginia Department of Game and Inland Fisheries (804) 367-1000
Size: 5,300 acres
Closest Town: Bassett

CENTRAL

63

REGION FIVE: SOUTHWESTERN HIGHLANDS

Nestled between West Virginia and Kentucky to the north and North Carolina to the south, the Southwestern Highlands region is one of striking beauty, diverse wildlife habitats, and superlatives. The Commonwealth's 2 highest points, Mount Rogers and Whitetop Mountain, are located in this region. Here is the largest canyon east of the Mississippi at Breaks Interstate Park, and the second-oldest river in the world, the New River.

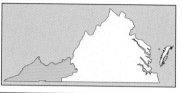

Photo, opposite page: sow black bear with cub. BILL LEA

WILDLIFE VIEWING SITES
49 Mountain Lake
50 New River
51 Little Wolf Creek Primitive Management Area
52 Big Walker Mountain Scenic Byway
53 Hungry Mother State Park
54 Grayson Highlands State Park
55 Virginia Creeper Trail
56 Mount Rogers
57 Clinch Mountain Wildlife Management Area
58 Breaks Interstate Park
59 High Knob
60 Elk Garden/Whitetop Mountain

Description: The University of Virginia uses Mountain Lake, spring-fed at an elevation of 3,875 feet, as a living laboratory. The region has long been recognized for biological diversity and dramatic scenery: northern hardwoods mixed with pine and hemlock, boreal woods, rocky outcroppings, a quaking bog, a virgin hemlock stand, and a bald atop Salt Pond Mountain.

Viewing Information: Mountain Lake, the Wilderness Conservancy at Mountain Lake, the University of Virginia's Mountain Lake Biological Station, and the 10,000-acre Forest Service wilderness area all offer abundant viewing opportunities. Where VA SR 700 intersects VA SR 613 at Mountain Lake, follow VA SR 613 north up the mountain. Drive slowly, or park and hike VA SR 613 or trails leading from it. Year-round, view red-tailed hawk, ruffed grouse, wild turkey, barred owl, pileated woodpecker, black-capped chickadee, cedar waxwing, white-tailed deer, and gray squirrel. Spring through fall, look for eastern box turtle, timber rattlesnake, northern copperhead, gray treefrog, Fowler's toad, and redback salamander. Black bear, bobcat, long-tailed weasel, and mink are also present, though difficult to see. Mountain laurel, rhododendron, and flame azalea bloom profusely. In Mountain Lake Wilderness, a popular 5-mile hike follows the Appalachian Trail from War Spur (Branch) to Wind Rock; park on VA SR 613, 3.2 miles (north) past Mountain Lake Hotel on the right, where the virgin hemlock stand is visible. Ruffed grouse, wild turkey, and black bear are present. During spring and fall between 10 a.m. and 2 p.m. on windy days at Wind Rock, see many migrating hawks.

Directions: *From Blacksburg, take U.S. Highway 460 west for 9 miles to VA SR 700. Turn right (north) and follow 7 miles to Mountain Lake.*

Ownership: USDA Forest Service (703) 552-4641; Wilderness Conservancy (703) 626-7121; or contact Appalachian Trail Conference (304) 535-6331.
Size: 13,200 acres
Closest Town: Blacksburg

The short, flutelike trill of the gray treefrog's call has been likened to the voice of the red-bellied woodpecker.
ADAM JONES

50 NEW RIVER

Description: Visitors are impressed with this wide, crystalline river and its backdrop of mountains. The New River is not new in geologic terms—it is the second-oldest river in the world after the Nile River in Egypt.

Viewing Information: Popular among swimmers and tubers, this section of the river has many edges and pools, and is uncommonly clear. Aquatic life is abundant and the best wildlife viewing is below the water surface. During the summer months, it is one of the best snorkeling waters in the Commonwealth; smallmouth bass, spotted bass, rock bass, redbreast sunfish, logperch, common carp, muskellunge, whitetail shiner, channel catfish, freshwater sponges, and mussels can be seen. *NATURAL AREA WITH NO FACILITIES.*

Directions: From Blacksburg, go west on VA SR 685 (Prices Fork Road) for 5 miles to Prices Fork. Make a right onto VA SR 652 and follow for 7 miles; go past McCoy. At the river, turn right onto VA SR 625 and follow until the river and the road are adjacent. Park in pull-offs along the river.

Ownership: Commonwealth of Virginia
Size: NA   **Closest Town:** McCoy

51 LITTLE WOLF CREEK PRIMITIVE MANAGEMENT AREA

Description: This exceptionally scenic hike along the Appalachian Trail parallels hemlock-bordered Little Wolf Creek and features thick rhododendron, many snags, and marshes created by beaver activity.

Viewing Information: Excellent viewing of beaver, muskrat, barred owl, bobwhite, wild turkey, wood duck, and reptiles and amphibians along the Appalachian Trail. For a longer loop hike (approximately 6 miles), follow the Appalachian Trail to High Water Trail. High Water Trail ends at VA SR 615; take a right onto VA SR 615 and hike for 0.25 mile, then take the Trail Boss Trail, on left, and hike 3.8 miles down (turn right at A.T. intersection), hike A.T. back to 615, turn right and return to parking area. *NATURAL AREA WITH NO FACILITIES.*

Directions: At junction of Interstate 77 and VA PR 42 near Bland (south of Bluefield, WV), travel west on VA PR 42 for 3 miles to VA SR 615. Turn right and follow for approximately 2.6 miles to Appalachian Trail crossing. Head south on the trail over the log footbridge. The crossing is most easily recognized by the log footbridge on the left-hand side. A parking area is located further down VA SR 615 on the left just before the one-lane bridge.

Ownership: USDA Forest Service (703) 228-5551 or contact Appalachian Trail Conference (304) 535-6331.
Size: 5-mile hike   **Closest Town:** Bland

SOUTHWESTERN HIGHLANDS

Description: *AUTO TOUR.* Big Walker Scenic Byway is a 16.2-mile driving tour through Bland and Wythe counties. Panoramic views, historical sites, a 100-foot observation tower with views of several states, hiking, and abundant wildlife viewing are available as the byway passes through the Jefferson National Forest. Little Wolf Creek Primitive Management Area (see site 51) is in the immediate vicinity of this scenic drive and the two combined make an excellent driving/hiking tour. Look for VA SR 615 on the left about 5 miles beyond the observation tower on U.S. Highway 52 (which is also VA PR 42 in this section) and follow directions from VA SR 615 to Little Wolf Creek.

Viewing Information: White-tailed deer, wild turkey, bobwhite, and red-tailed hawk may be seen during the drive. Please use caution while viewing wildlife from a moving vehicle. An excellent place for a short wildlife hike is the Wetland Nature Walk off of VA SR 717, identified by a sign with the binocular logo. Look for beaver, red-winged blackbird, white-tailed deer, and downy woodpecker. A 0.5-mile trail at the Buck Astin Home Site meanders through 3 vegetative types: open grass, hemlock/hardwood riparian, and upland hardwood. Along the trail in summer, look for American goldfinch, eastern bluebird, and eastern meadowlark; in winter look for cedar waxwing and black-capped chickadee.

Directions: *At junction of Interstate 77 and VA SR 717 (5 miles north of Wytheville and south of Bluefield, WV), travel west 6 miles on VA SR 717 to U.S. Highway 52. Turn right and ascend Big Walker Mountain. Continue on U.S. 52 until it intersects Interstate 77, marking the end of the scenic byway.*

Ownership: USDA Forest Service (703) 228-5551
Size: 16.2-mile drive   **Closest Town:** Wytheville

Red squirrels are sometimes called "boomers," "pine squirrels," and even the "fairy diddle." The characteristic white eye-ring is an excellent field identification mark.

JOHN GERLACH

53 | HUNGRY MOTHER STATE PARK

Description: Steep slopes and woodlands surround 108-acre Hungry Mother Lake. Eight trails lead wildlife viewers to serene lake vistas, mixed deciduous woodlands, laurel and rhododendron thickets, hemlock ravines, and wetlands.

Viewing Information: Good chance to see beaver during spring and fall early mornings and late afternoons. Excellent songbird viewing, especially in the woodlands and hemlock ravine. On spring mornings, look for several warbler species: the black-and-white, black-throated blue, blackburnian, chestnut-sided, Cape May, and others. Woodchuck, raccoon, chipmunk, and fox squirrel might be seen in the area around the Hungry Mother Boat Ramp. Many species of waterfowl can be seen on the lake year-round. Look for common loon and great blue and green-backed heron in or along the water on spring and fall mornings.

Directions: From Interstate 81, exit north on VA PR 16 at Marion. Follow park signs and stay on VA PR 16 north for 3.7 miles to park entrance.

Ownership: Virginia Department of Conservation and Recreation (703) 783-3422
Size: 2,200 acres
Closest Town: Marion

54 | GRAYSON HIGHLANDS STATE PARK

Description: Spruce-fir forests, northern hardwoods, sphagnum bogs, rocky outcroppings, and mountain balds set against a backdrop of rugged mountains make Grayson Highlands one of Virginia's premiere state parks. Elevations in the park range from 3,800 to 5,100 feet; in places, Grayson Highlands looks more like a Canadian park.

Viewing Information: Excellent white-tailed deer viewing early mornings and late evenings year-round. Black bear amble across the mountain slopes. Good chance of seeing wild turkey, ruffed grouse, and eastern and New England cottontail along roadsides. In winter look for cedar waxwing in the spruce forest. In summer, red-tailed, broad-winged, and red-shouldered hawks grace the sky, as does the American kestrel. Numerous songbirds in summer. Profuse wildflowers in spring—catawba rhododendron on balds, pink lady's slipper in hardwood stands, and trillium on shaded hardwood slopes.

Directions: From Interstate 81 in Marion (exit 45), take VA PR 16 south for approximately 23 miles. At junction of VA PR 16 and U.S. Highway 58, travel west on U.S. 58; go 8 miles to park entrance.

Ownership: Virginia Department of Conservation and Recreation (703) 579-7092
Size: 5,000 acres
Closest Town: Volney

SOUTHWESTERN HIGHLANDS

Description: A converted railroad bed, the Virginia Creeper Trail is a 34-mile hiking, biking, equestrian and wildlife-watching trail climbing moderately from Abingdon to Whitetop. A National Recreation Trail, the footpath passes along the South Holston Reservoir and through Mount Rogers National Recreation Area.

Viewing Information: Excellent songbird and wildflower displays. Year-round, look for songbirds such as black-capped chickadee, dark-eyed junco, American goldfinch, and rufous-sided towhee. In summer, observe chestnut-sided, Canada, and black-throated blue warbler. In winter, cedar waxwings are present. Five species of owls occur: great horned, barred, eastern screech, saw-whet, and long-eared. In spring, painted trillium, bloodroot, spring beauty, bellwort, Solomon's-seal, and foamflower bloom. Rhododendron, Virginia dayflower, ditch stonecrop, and pipsissewa bloom in early summer, and in late summer look for pink Joe-Pye weed and tall ironweed. Beaver can sometimes be seen along Berry Creek. Several beaver dams can be seen as the trail parallels the creek. Signs of beaver include the chewed trees and a warning "slap," caused by the tail against the water while submerging. Look for beaver late in the day and into the evening.

Directions: The trailhead is near the corner of A Street SE and Green Springs Road in Abingdon. Other access points are Watauga Road; VA SR 677, approximately 4 miles east of Abingdon; Alvarado; Damascus; and in Mount Rogers National Recreation Area and Whitetop.

Ownership: Various; (703) 676-2282 or (800)-435-3440
Size: 34-mile trail
Closest Town: Abingdon

Catawba rhododendron is a member of the heath family. The brilliant flowers of the heath family inspired poet Ralph Waldo Emerson to write, "Tell them, dear, that if eyes were made for seeing...beauty is its own excuse for being." JOHN SHAW

Description: The highest point in Virginia, Mount Rogers stands at a majestic 5,729 feet. The Mount Rogers National Recreation Area boasts such diverse habitats as rocky outcroppings, Fraser fir, red spruce, dense patches of blueberries, grassy mountain balds, and thousands of acres of rhododendron. The Fraser fir stands in the Mount Rogers NRA High Country are the northernmost natural Fraser fir stands and the only naturally-occurring stands in Virginia.

Viewing Information: Wildlife viewing in the High Country is best on the Appalachian Trail and Wilburn Ridge Trail along Wilburn Ridge. From the Massie Gap parking area in Grayson Highlands State Park, follow the Rhododendron Gap Trail 0.5 mile to the Appalachian Trail. Hike south along the A.T. for 0.5 mile and enter the Mount Rogers NRA. Continue south along the A.T. and enjoy the magnificent views from the east side of Wilburn Ridge. As an alternative, hike the Wilburn Ridge Trail along the summit of Wilburn Ridge. This blue-blazed trail leaves the A.T. and then rejoins it after 0.6 mile. Rhododendron Gap is 2.5 miles from Massie Gap, with magnificent views from the cliffs. Many hawks, including the broad-winged, red-tailed, Cooper's, and sharp-shinned, soar overhead or perch in trees. Look for hawks between mid-morning and early afternoon. Search the rock cliffs around Wilburn Ridge for peregrine falcons. Songbird viewing is excellent; from spring to fall in early mornings spot rufous-sided towhee, indigo bunting, American goldfinch, eastern wood pewee, and dark-eyed junco. Listen for owls at night. This is an especially good area for the saw-whet owl. White-tailed deer browse the forest edge in mornings and early evenings, and black bear frequent berry patches in summer. Bobcats may appear around cliffs, but require effort to see. Flame azalea, rhododendron, and mountain laurel provide brilliant shows between May and June.

Directions: *From Interstate 81 in Marion (exit 45), take VA PR 16 south for approximately 23 miles. At junction of VA PR 16 and U.S. Highway 58, travel west on U.S. 58 for 8 miles to Grayson Highlands State Park. Proceed to Massie Gap parking area.*

Ownership: USDA Forest Service, (703) 783-5196; or contact Appalachian Trail Conference (304) 535-6331.

Size: 5,000 acres

Closest Town: Marion

SOUTHWESTERN HIGHLANDS

The Mount Rogers region supports many rare species, including the only naturally-occurring Fraser fir stand in Virginia, and the Weller's salamander, one of the Commonwealth's rarest amphibians.

FRED CRAMER

71

Description: Clinch Mountain is not only the Virginia Game and Inland Fisheries' largest management area, but also one of its most biologically diverse. Ranging from picturesque Big Tumbling Creek and many beaver ponds in the lower elevations to the red spruce forest on 4,600-foot Beartown Mountain, the area is a showcase for sweeping views and a multitude of wildlife.

Viewing Information: Viewing opportunities range from auto-touring along VA SR 747 to hiking gated administrative roads and boating on 300-acre Laurel Bed Lake. White-tailed deer abound, as do ruffed grouse, wild turkey, owls, woodchuck, raccoon, chipmunk, squirrels, and cottontail rabbit. Wood duck and mallard can be viewed in November on Laurel Bed Lake; the black duck, bufflehead, and pied-billed grebe also use the lake in fall. Spotted and solitary sandpiper frequent the lake in summer along with great blue heron; a bald eagle might be seen here as well. At dawn and dusk between April and September watch for 3 species of bat—the little brown, eastern pipistrelle, and big brown—near the lights at the depot facility. Beaver are fairly abundant in the marshes and Laurel Bed Lake. Songbird viewing in the shrublands and deciduous forest is excellent. *PUBLIC HUNTING AREA: CONTACT MANAGER FOR AFFECTED AREAS.*

Directions: *From Interstate 81, take Exit 35 at Chilhowie to VA PR 107 north to Saltville (8 miles). Go left on VA PR 91 to VA SR 634 (0.25 mile). Go right (north) on VA SR 634 for 1 mile to VA SR 613 in Allison Gap. Turn left (west) and proceed 3.5 miles to VA SR 747. Turn right on VA SR 747 which leads to viewing area.*

Ownership: Virginia Department of Game and Inland Fisheries (703) 944-3434
Size: 15,000 of 25,500 total acres
Closest Town: Saltville

Wildlife management efforts by the Virginia Department of Game and Inland Fisheries have brought back declining wild turkey populations. LEONARD LEE RUE III

Description: Along the Virginia-Kentucky border the Russell Fork River at Breaks Interstate Park has carved the largest canyon east of the Mississippi. More than 5 miles long and 1,600 feet deep, it is often referred to as the Grand Canyon of the South. The sheer rock walls, deep canyon, and rich deciduous and mixed forests are the grandeur that is Breaks.

Viewing Information: White-tailed deer are seen year-round in the early morning and early evening along forest edges and in open, grassy areas. Cottontail rabbit, wild turkey, gray squirrel, white-breasted nuthatch, Carolina chickadee, Carolina wren, pileated woodpecker, ruffed grouse, red-tailed hawk, and tufted titmouse are also year-round residents. From April to September, look for the broad-winged hawk, wood thrush, summer tanager, wood duck, and indigo bunting. Greater and lesser yellowlegs might be seen on the pond in April/May and July. Little brown and big brown bat can be seen flying at dusk. During spring and summer, gray tree frog (call is a short flutelike trill) and mountain chorus frog (mating call is a harsh, raspy "reek") might be seen, but most likely heard.

Directions: From junction of Interstate 81 and VA PR 80 (south of Meadowview), travel north on VA PR 80 for approximately 65 miles.

Ownership: Jointly owned by Virginia and Kentucky (703) 865-4413
Size: 4,500 acres
Closest Town: Haysi

Pileated woodpeckers feed on insects found in dead stumps and trees.
BILL LEA

SOUTHWESTERN HIGHLANDS

Description: Drive to the top of 4,160-foot High Knob and take a 0.25-mile walk to the lookout tower for 360-degree panoramic views. From the tower, 5 states can be seen: Kentucky, West Virginia, North Carolina, Tennessee, and Virginia.

Viewing Information: Very impressive viewing of broad-winged hawk migration in fall, as hundreds pass by. View from the observation tower and open area around tower. At times, many of these hawks can be seen together as they usually migrate in flocks. Identify this bird by the whitish underwing and bands on its tail—the 2 white bands are as wide as the 3 black bands (note: immature birds have more bands). The hawks are on their way to Central and South America for the winter. A 1.1-mile trail from the tower down to High Knob Lake offers additional birding opportunities. In winter, resident birds, such as tufted titmouse, Carolina chickadee, and golden-crowned kinglet remain. In spring, many songbirds are present, though some are difficult to see. In the early morning, look for warbler species: the Canada, black-and-white, magnolia, chestnut-sided, black-throated blue, and cerulean. Also present are the Louisiana waterthrush, American redstart, solitary vireo, rose-breasted grosbeak, scarlet tanager, and ovenbird. In warmer months, mountain dusky salamanders, ravine salamanders, and red-spotted newts (efts) are present in the woodlands.

Directions: From Norton, take VA SR 619 south up the mountain for 3.7 miles. Turn left onto Forest Road 238 and follow it east for 0.3 mile to the tower entrance on the right.

Ownership: USDA Forest Service (703) 328-2931
Size: 3 acres   **Closest Town:** Norton

Scarlet tanagers summer in Virginia and winter in South America. Male scarlet tanagers are red during the summer; in winter they look similar to the females, which, year-round, have dull green backs and a green-yellow underside. ROB SIMPSON

Description: The rocky outcroppings interspersed throughout expansive mountain balds at Elk Garden look more like a scene from Montana than Virginia. Hike the Appalachian Trail to view wildlife. For a lesson in ecology, drive to the top of Whitetop Mountain through a deciduous hardwood forest, northern hardwood forest, subalpine beech forest, northern red spruce forest, and mountaintop bald. The views from Whitetop are awesome.

Viewing Information: Drive VA SR 600 in early mornings during warmer months to see white-tailed deer, gray fox, eastern cottontail, and woodchuck; at night, drive slowly for possible glimpses of opossum, raccoon, gray fox, black bear, and bobcat. Please use caution while driving. Look for red squirrel in the spruce stand off Forest Road 89 during the day. Hawks, owls, and bobcats in the area eat red squirrels, sometimes called boomers. Between April and September, look for hawks: red-tailed, broad-winged, and red-shouldered. In the open balds in summer, look for rufous-sided towhee, dark-eyed junco, and robin. Spot the Canada warbler at the edge of spruce forests. Colorful flower shows abound. In the spring, fringed phacelia, trout lily, bellwort, and bluets bloom; in early summer bee balm and bluebead lily bloom. *NATURAL AREA WITH NO FACILITIES.*

Directions: From Abingdon, take U.S. Highway 58 east about 20 miles to VA SR 603 near Konnarock. Bear left on VA SR 603 for 2 miles and then make a right (south) onto VA SR 600 (stop at the Elk Garden parking to see Elk Garden). Continue on VA SR 600 for 1 mile to Forest Road 89 on right which goes to the top of the mountain.

Ownership: USDA Forest Service, (703) 783-5196; or contact the Appalachian Trail Conference, (304) 535-6331.

Size: 5,000 acres **Closest Town:** Abingdon

Two species of fox occur in Virginia, the red fox and the slightly smaller gray fox. The gray fox, pictured here, prefers more wooded habitats, while the red fox favors more open habitats, such as old fields and croplands.

BILL LEA

SOUTHWESTERN HIGHLANDS

REGION SIX: SHENANDOAH

Native Americans named this region "Shenandoah," meaning "daughter of the stars," while early pioneers and visitors proclaimed it a land of milk and honey. Bordered on the east by the Blue Ridge Mountains and the Allegheny Mountains on the west, it is perhaps one of the most beautiful regions in the world. Long parallel mountain ridges running generally northeast to southwest characterize the region. Bisecting the region lengthwise is the Valley of Virginia; the Shenandoah Valley is located in the northern section, the Valley of the James is to the southwest of the Shenandoah Valley, and the Roanoke Valley is at the southern end.

Photo, opposite page: white-tailed deer. LEN RUE, JR.

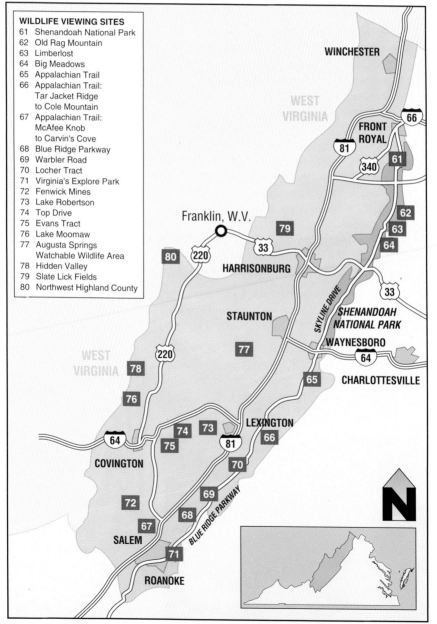

WILDLIFE VIEWING SITES
61 Shenandoah National Park
62 Old Rag Mountain
63 Limberlost
64 Big Meadows
65 Appalachian Trail
66 Appalachian Trail:
    Tar Jacket Ridge
    to Cole Mountain
67 Appalachian Trail:
    McAfee Knob
    to Carvin's Cove
68 Blue Ridge Parkway
69 Warbler Road
70 Locher Tract
71 Virginia's Explore Park
72 Fenwick Mines
73 Lake Robertson
74 Top Drive
75 Evans Tract
76 Lake Moomaw
77 Augusta Springs
    Watchable Wildlife Area
78 Hidden Valley
79 Slate Lick Fields
80 Northwest Highland County

Description: Shenandoah National Park is one of Virginia's premiere wildlife viewing locales. From Front Royal in the north to Waynesboro in the south, the park encompasses almost 200,000 acres of the Blue Ridge Mountains and showcases abundant and diverse wildlife resources. Skyline Drive, a 105-mile scenic drive, runs the length of the park, following the high ridgetops. The 102 miles of Appalachian Trail in the park roughly parallel Skyline Drive, crossing it at many points. Wildlife viewing experiences range from auto touring, bicycling, and horseback riding to hiking paved trails and backpacking to remote wildlands.

Viewing Information: Shenandoah is home to 205 species of birds, over 40 species of mammals, 26 species of reptiles, 24 species of amphibians, 1,100 species of flowering plants, 100 species of trees, 47 species of ferns and fern-allies, and numerous species of mosses and liverworts. Almost 6,000 white-tailed deer and 300 to 600 black bear live in the park. Deer are easily spotted year-round in open fields and along the forest edge early mornings and late evenings; lucky visitors may see a bear between April and December (bears hibernate during the coldest months of the year). In fall, climb to a rocky peak and watch for migrating hawks such as red-tailed, Cooper's, broad-winged, sharp-shinned, and others. Peregrine falcons are present spring through fall, but rare; the highest peaks offer the best chances of sighting one. During the day, look for woodpeckers, gray squirrel, bobwhite, wild turkey, and ruffed grouse. Evening brings out raccoon, opossum, gray fox, bobcat, skunk, and bats. Flowers bloom profusely between spring and late summer. Particularly noticeable are dogwood, azalea, and mountain laurel. *NO MOUNTAIN BICYCLING IS ALLOWED ON TRAILS.*

Directions: Four intersections mark entrances to the park. From the north: U.S. Highway 340 at the southern limit of Front Royal; U.S. 211 at Thornton Gap; U.S. 33 at Swift Run Gap; and Rockfish Gap at I-64 and U.S. 250.

Ownership: National Park Service (703) 999-2243
Size: 195,525 acres   **Closest Towns:** Front Royal (north), Waynesboro (south), Luray (central), Sperryville (central), Elkton (central)

Stooping at speeds of up to 180 m.p.h., peregrine falcons feed on songbirds, pelagic birds, rock doves, and many species of waterfowl. This immature peregrine has just taken a male wood duck.

LEN RUE, JR.

62 OLD RAG MOUNTAIN

Description: Once called "Old Raggedy," Old Rag Mountain is Virginia's most popular mountain hike, and perhaps Virginia's grandest mountain. Standing separate from the continuous Blue Ridge chain, it is a very rocky mountain with many granite outcroppings, cliffs, and vertical walls. Panoramic views abound along the trail, and especially from the summit.

Viewing Information: Along the trail, year-round, white-tailed deer and wild turkey sometimes make early morning and late afternoon appearances, mainly on less crowded days. Black bears are sometimes seen in the warmer months. Mid-day during fall, particularly mid-September, migrating hawks can be observed, such as red-tailed, Cooper's, sharp-shinned, and broad-winged. Red-tailed hawks are year-round residents as well. On warm days look for them catching a free ride in thermals, columns of rising warm air, along with ravens and turkey vultures. Timber rattlesnake and copperhead are active from mid-May to September. The flower show in spring is equal to the grandeur of the mountain: redbud, dogwood, azalea, and trillium splash the forest with garnet, whites, reds, and pinks. The summit is approximately 2.7 miles via the Ridge Trail. *NATURAL AREA WITH NO FACILITIES. THE HIKE TO THE SUMMIT IS QUITE STEEP.*

Directions: *From Madison, take VA PR 231 north for 9 miles to Peola Mills, turning left onto VA SR 602. Travel for 1.5 miles and turn left onto VA SR 707. Continue 1 mile to Nethers, then bear left onto VA SR 600 to parking area.*

Ownership: National Park Service (703) 999-2243
Size: 2.7-mile summit trail.
Closest Town: Madison

Old Rag Mountain. BILL LEA

SHENANDOAH

63 LIMBERLOST

Description: The stand of virgin hemlock at Limberlost forms such a thick canopy that it is seldom bright in the forest, even at mid-day. The large, 300 to 400 year-old hemlocks were spared in the late nineteenth century when George Freeman Pollock, a major proponent for the establishment of Shenandoah National Park, paid a lumberman $10 a tree NOT to cut the grove of 100 giant trees. The easy hike to Limberlost is 1.5 miles round-trip.

Viewing Information: White-tailed deer and black bear are sometimes seen in the early morning and late evening along the trail. Wild turkey might be viewed year-round, but seem to be most watchable in winter. Cottontail rabbit, and gray and red squirrel are present. The red squirrel is smaller than its cousin, the eastern gray squirrel, and is more often heard before it is seen. Listen for its ratchetlike call and chattering; then look for it sitting on a tree branch. In summer identify the red squirrel from the gray by the distinct black line separating its dark back, and white underside. This is an excellent spot to see the blackburnian warbler. The shady, moist forests provide excellent growing conditions for Indian pipe, a saprophytic plant with a white nodding flower that blooms in summer.

Directions: From junction of U.S. Highway 211 and Skyline Drive (east of Luray), travel south, or from U.S. 33 and Skyline Drive (east of Elkton) travel north on Skyline Drive to Limberlost Trail parking area at milepost 43.

Ownership: National Park Service (703) 999-2243
Size: 25 acres   **Closest Town:** Luray

The blackburnian warbler can be seen in Virginia only during the warmer months; it summers in western Virginia and winters from Costa Rica to Peru. ROB SIMPSON

Description: A picturesque, 100-acre treeless area located on the east side of Skyline Drive (milepost 51), Big Meadows has an uncertain history. Two prominent theories as to its origin include the following: (1) it was maintained at least in part through grazing by large ungulates such as bison and elk, or (2) it was established and sustained with fire by Indians for the purposes of berry production and maintenance of hunting grounds. The National Park Service now maintains the area in an open state through selective pruning.

Viewing Information: Possibly the best locale in Virginia to see white-tailed deer year-round. Hike any one of the small footpaths through the meadow early in the morning or early evening to see bucks, does, and fawns feeding. During the day, white-tailed deer conceal themselves in thick cover but become active late in the day and early in the morning to feed on grasses, wild fruits, twigs, leaves, and acorns. Bucks begin growing a new set of antlers each spring and by early fall attain full growth. There are 2 main types of antlers: (1) spikes - small main beams with no prongs - are peglike and usually a yearling's first set of antlers; (2) classic branched antlers. Rutting, a stage of sexual excitement marked by bucks fighting and sparring with each other, takes place between late October and early November; breeding takes place between November and December. Antlers fall off after the fall rut. One to 4, but usually 2, fawns are born in May and June. Fawns are mottled with white spots for camouflage, simulating flecks of sunlight on a forest floor.

Directions: From junction of U.S. Highway 211 and Skyline Drive (east of Luray) travel south, or from the junction of U.S. 33 and Skyline Drive (east of Elkton) travel north on Skyline Drive to Big Meadows (milepost 51).

Ownership: National Park Service (703) 999-2243
Size: More than 100 acres   **Closest Town**: Luray, Elkton

The open, parklike setting at Big Meadows is excellent white-tailed deer habitat.

ROB SIMPSON

SHENANDOAH

Description: The Appalachian National Scenic Trail (A.T.) is a continuous marked footpath traversing the Appalachian mountain chain from Georgia to Maine—approximately 2,155 miles. About 545 miles, one-fourth of the entire trail, is located in Virginia. The A.T. is not only a footpath, but a corridor of land averaging 1,000 feet in width along the crest of the Appalachian Mountains. Though the dominant habitat along the trail is eastern hardwood forest, many sections of the trail include open pastures, rock outcroppings, spruce-fir forests, high mountain streams, waterfalls, and wetlands.

Viewing Information: The A.T. in Virginia passes through a wide array of habitat types and elevations, ranging from less than 800 feet at the crossing of the James River to nearly 5,700 feet near the summit of Mount Rogers. Many species can be viewed, including white-tailed deer, wild turkey, ruffed grouse, turkey vulture, migrating hawks, bobcat, gray fox, opossum, black bear, raccoon, great horned owl, eastern screech-owl, barred owl, short-eared owl, pileated, downy and hairy woodpecker, a wide variety of songbirds, eastern painted turtle, eastern box turtle, eastern spadefoot, American and Fowler's toad, gray treefrog, spring peeper, upland chorus frog, pickerel frog, wood frog, eastern hognose snake, eastern milk snake, and timber rattlesnake.

Directions: Most sections of the trail can be reached from trailheads where the trail intersects state and local highways and park and forest roads. Contact the Appalachian Trail Conference (304) 535-6331 for guide books and maps. See sites 5, 49, 51, 56, 60, 66, and 67.

Ownership: Managed and maintained by the Appalachian Trail Conference (304) 535-6331 and member trail clubs in cooperation with the National Park Service, USDA Forest Service and others.

Size: 545 miles in Virginia **Closest Town:** Many

Bobcats are secretive, and without a great deal of effort, difficult to see. However, chance sightings occasionally occur along the Appalachian Trail. BILL LEA

66 APPALACHIAN TRAIL: TAR JACKET RIDGE TO COLE MOUNTAIN

Description: The open, grassy, and shrubby areas along this section of the Appalachian Trail east of Buena Vista are known as "balds," found on many mountaintops throughout the southeastern United States. The open areas and rocky outcroppings provide panoramic vistas and unimpeded wildlife viewing.

Viewing Information: By foot from VA SR 755, follow the Appalachian Trail, distinguished by a white blaze mark about every 100 feet, north to Tar Jacket Ridge, or south to Cole Mountain. The balds are used as hunting grounds by many species of hawk— red-tailed, broad-winged, Cooper's, and sharp-shinned. On fall mid-afternoons, migrating hawks soar over the ridges, riding thermals. A peregrine falcon hacking site is nearby, and a few resident birds are present.

Directions: At the junction of Interstate 81 and U.S. Highway 60 west of Buena Vista (Rockbridge County), travel east on U.S. 60 for 11.5 miles to VA SR 634 (Coffey Town Road) in Amherst County. Turn left (north) and follow for 2 miles to VA SR 755 (Ham Kerr Road). Turn right; the road ends at the parking area.

Ownership: USDA Forest Service; contact Appalachian Trail Conference (304) 535-6331
Size: 5-mile-long trail
Closest Town: Buena Vista

67 APPALACHIAN TRAIL: MCAFEE KNOB TO CARVIN'S COVE

Description: This section of the Appalachian Trail extends 23 miles from VA PR 311 on the southern end to Carvin's Cove in the north, and can be accessed from U.S. Highway 220 or VA PR 311. Tinker Cliffs, roughly halfway along this route, and McAfee Knob, about 3.5 miles north of the southern terminus, provide sweeping mountain views. The northern section of McAfee Knob is a large rock garden called the Devil's Kitchen.

Viewing Information: Many hawks are viewed during fall migration during mid-day. Turkey vulture, ruffed grouse, black bear, white-tailed deer, and eastern box turtle are also present. *NATURAL AREA WITH NO FACILITIES.*

Directions: To reach the north end of the trail: at the junction of Interstate 81 and U.S. Highway 220 (exit 44, U.S. 220, just north of Roanoke), take the first left off of U.S. 220 into parking area for the Trail, hike south. To reach the south end of the trail: At the junction of Interstate 81, VA PR 311 and VA PR 419 (exit 41, just west of Roanoke), travel north on VA PR 311 for 6 miles to the A.T., parking area on the left, hike north.

Ownership: National Park Service, contact the Appalachian Trail Conference (304) 535-6331
Size: 23 miles of A.T.   **Closest Town:** Daleville

SHENANDOAH

Description: The Blue Ridge Parkway is an extraordinary mountain highway 469 miles long, linking the Shenandoah National Park to Great Smoky Mountains National Park. Slightly less than half of the parkway, 216 miles, is located in Virginia. Dramatic changes in elevation and diverse habitats such as Appalachian hardwood forests, spruce forests, coves, hollows, and balds provide for wide biological diversity and wildlife viewing.

Viewing Information: White-tailed deer, wild turkey, turkey vulture, bobwhite, several owl and hawk species, woodchuck, raccoon, chipmunk, gray and red squirrel, gray fox, and black bear live along the parkway. Bear are seen only occasionally, and hibernate during the coldest part of the year. Several species of songbirds live in the area year-round: Carolina chickadee, tufted titmouse, white-breasted nuthatch, and Carolina wren. In spring, many birds migrate back from their wintering grounds to nest and breed. Look for warbler species: the Canada, black-and-white, black-throated green, chestnut-sided, black-throated blue, hooded, blackburnian, and worm-eating. The parkway is renowned for its bounteous flowers. The great variation in elevation ensures blooms from early spring to late summer. A sampling of flowers includes rhododendron, dogwood, redbud, daisies, wild rose, mountain laurel, meadow salsify, black-eyed susan, and turkeybeard.

Directions: The Blue Ridge Parkway follows the mountain chain from Rockfish Gap south into North Carolina. The Parkway begins at the junction of Interstate 64 and U.S. Highway 250 (east of Waynesboro). The Parkway can also be accessed by U.S. Highways 60, 460, 220, 58, as well as Interstate 77 and numerous state roads.

Ownership: National Park Service (704) 298-0398
Size: 216-mile parkway
Closest Town: Many

Turkey vultures have a wingspan of 6 feet and are a common sight throughout Virginia. Adults have red heads while juveniles have darker heads. JOHN NETHERTON

Description: Dubbed "Warbler Road" by Virginia birders, this locale on the Glenwood Ranger District is considered one of the best warbler viewing areas in the entire Blue Ridge. The drive is exceptionally beautiful as well. Following largely unpaved (but easily passable during the warmer months) forest roads from the valley floor along Wildcat Mountain to the Blue Ridge Parkway, a variety of habitats are traversed. Experienced viewers can see 20 or more breeding species of warbler.

Viewing Information: In early May at the lower levels search for the pine, parula, and hooded warbler. Continuing the ascent, look for the worm-eating, golden-winged, blue-winged, and Kentucky warbler. Golden- and blue-winged warbler are most likely seen in and around recently-clearcut areas. On the higher elevations approaching the parkway, look for the cerulean, black-throated blue, black-throated green, chestnut-sided, black-and-white, Canada, and blackburnian warbler.

Directions: North of Buchanan at junction of Interstate 81 and VA SR 614, take VA SR 614 east for 3 miles through Arcadia to Forest Road 59. FR 59 is the first road on the left after entering the National Forest (there is a sign for North Creek Campground). Turn left onto FR 59 and drive to FR 768 (Thomas Mtn. Rd.) on the left (there is a sign at this junction for Cave Mountain Lake and the Parkway). Turn left onto FR 768 and continue to FR 812 (Parker's Gap Road). Turn right and continue to the Blue Ridge Parkway. FR 812 enters the parkway in the corner of the parking lot at Sunset Field (Apple Orchard Falls Trail).

Ownership: USDA Forest Service (703) 291-2188
Size: 14-mile drive   **Closest Town:** Buchanan

In spring, the chestnut-sided warbler can be identified by its yellow crown and brown or "chestnut" sides. During fall look for its olive crown and white underside, as pictured above. ROB SIMPSON

SHENANDOAH

70 LOCHER TRACT

Description: The exceptionally beautiful Locher Tract, bordered on the north by the James River and by the James River Face National Wilderness on the south, offers river frontage, old fields, pasture fields, pond, hardwood forest, and beaver swamp for uncrowded wildlife viewing.

Viewing Information: From the parking area, hike along the Balcony Falls Trail in early mornings or late afternoons in summer for a chance to see white-tailed deer, songbirds (Carolina chickadee, white-breasted nuthatch, eastern bluebird, blue-gray gnatcatcher) and wild turkey. There is also a mowed loop trail through the area. In the pond or James River, chances are good of seeing wood duck, Canada goose, and mallard. The James River Face Wilderness is 1.6 miles away. *NATURAL AREA WITH NO FACILITIES.*

Directions: *From junction of U.S. Highway 11 and VA PR 130 in Natural Bridge, take VA PR 130 east 2.5 miles to VA SR 759. Turn right and proceed 1 mile to VA SR 782. Turn left onto VA SR 782 which becomes Forest Road 3093; parking area is at the road's end.*

Ownership: USDA Forest Service (703) 291-2188
Size: 90 acres   **Closest Towns:** Natural Bridge, Glasgow

71 VIRGINIA'S EXPLORE PARK

Description: Situated along 2.5 miles of the palatial Roanoke River Gorge, the park consists of natural wildlands, wildlife corridors, stunning shale cliffs, and wildlife viewing facilities interspersed with environmental educational facilities, including a frontier settlement, a North American wilderness zoological park, and an environmental education center.

Viewing Information: Warmer months provide excellent viewing along the river corridor and floodplain of fish, white-tailed deer, muskrat, waterfowl, beaver, kingfisher, and possibly in the evening, gray fox. Look year-round during daylight for the red-tailed, Cooper's, sharp-shinned and red-shouldered hawk along the forest edge and upland meadow; in evenings find barred and great horned owl. Bullfrog, spicebush swallowtail and tiger swallowtail are found in the pond and bordering open areas.

Directions: *Exit the Blue Ridge Parkway at milepost 115 onto Rutrough Road; turn left and go 1 mile to park. From Interstate 581 in Roanoke, take Elm Avenue east. Turn right onto 13th Street and left onto Riverland Road. Turn left again almost immediately onto Rutrough Road and proceed 4.5 miles; park is on the left.*

Ownership: Virginia Recreational Facilities Authority (703) 427-3107
Size: 1,200 acres
Closest Town: Roanoke

72 FENWICK MINES

Description: Focal points include open pit mines, foundations of old mining structures, nature trails, a beaver swamp, hardened barrier-free trails, and boardwalks through wetlands.

Viewing Information: White-tailed deer, gray squirrel, Carolina chickadee, white-breasted nuthatch, eastern bluebird, pileated woodpecker, rufous-sided towhee, and wild turkey are present year-round. During spring and summer, in early morning or late afternoon, hike near the fish pond or the wetland trail for potential glimpses of beaver and wood duck. In spring and summer, many songbirds appear: wood thrush, pine warbler, worm-eating warbler, and blue-gray gnatcatcher.

Directions: From Interstate 81, take exit 141 to VA PR 311 north to New Castle. From New Castle take VA SR 615 east for 5 miles to VA SR 611. Turn left and proceed for 0.1 mile to VA SR 685 and turn right. Follow to the mines' 2 parking areas on the right. A shelter and picnic area is found 0.4 mile farther up VA SR 685.

Ownership: USDA Forest Service (703) 864-5195
Size: 40 acres   **Closest Town:** New Castle

73 LAKE ROBERTSON

Description: Fourteen miles west of Lexington, in one of the most scenic regions in the entire Commonwealth, is 31-acre Lake A. Willis Robertson. Several trails traverse this 581-acre tract abutting the base of steep mountains.

Viewing Information: Fall and early winter are the best viewing times; schedule trips around hunting seasons. A variety of waterfowl use the lake during fall migration. From spring to fall, great blue and green-backed heron can be seen during the day and beaver and muskrat might be seen during evenings in the lake. *PUBLIC HUNTING AREA; PLEASE CHECK WITH MANAGER FOR AFFECTED AREAS.*

Directions: From Lexington, take VA PR 251 south (west) 10 miles to VA SR 770. Make a left and follow signs to the lake entrance on right.

Ownership: Virginia Department of Game and Inland Fisheries (703) 463-4164
Size: 581 acres   **Closest Town:** Lexington

SHENANDOAH

Description: High along the ridgetop on the border of Allegheny and Rockbridge counties is unpaved Forest Road 447, also known as Top Drive. With sweeping views, sometimes from both sides of the road, this is Skyline Drive without the crowds.

Viewing Information: Reaching Top Drive is slightly difficult as FR 447 and VA SR 770 are unpaved, rutted in places, and sometimes double back. However, once reached, Top Drive is very well maintained and fairly level as it traverses the ridge. Because Top Drive is somewhat remote, wildlife viewing here is very good. It is also one of the best mountain bike routes in the state. Look for white-tailed deer, wild turkey, red-tailed hawk, and ruffed grouse year-round. During fall, migrating hawks can be viewed from open areas and rocky outcroppings, especially in September. During summer, many warblers nest along the ridges. *USE CAUTION ON VA SR 770. NATURAL AREA WITH NO FACILITIES. PUBLIC HUNTING AREA: PLEASE CHECK WITH DISTRICT RANGER OFFICE FOR AFFECTED AREAS.*

Directions: From Interstate 64 west of Lexington, take Forest Road 447 (Top Drive) via Exit 43 (Goshen Exit) to the ridge top accessing North Mountain Overlook. If approaching from I-64 East, take Exit 35 (Longdale Exit) to U.S. Highway 60 west for approximately 0.5 mile. Turn left onto VA SR 770 and bear left at summit onto FR 447, traveling north to the North Mountain Overlook.

Ownership: USDA Forest Service (703) 962-2214
Size: 2,350 acres; drive 7.5 miles long
Closest Town: Clifton Forge

Finding signs of wildlife, like this deer jaw, is a rewarding part of spending time in the outdoors. Wildlife biologists use the jaw to age deer. CUB KAHN

Description: This former farm is located on the banks of the Cowpasture River, an idyllic, crystal-clear shallow stream. A large field borders the river, gently ascending to higher ridges of mixed upland oak and pine forests.

Viewing Information: The river's clarity offers ideal viewing of aquatic life, especially smallmouth bass, bluegill, rock bass, beaver, and snapping turtle. Year-round on the shores, look for great blue heron, and in the summer, green-backed heron. View wood duck and mallard during spring and summer on the river. Red-tailed hawk and American kestrel use the large fields as hunting grounds during daytime, while the great horned, eastern screech, and barred owl hunt the fields and forests at night. Look for eastern harvest mice, white-footed mice, and cottontail rabbit in the fields and along the forest edge; hawks and owls are looking for them, too. The fields also sustain killdeer (spring-summer), American woodcock (spring-fall), and bobwhite (year-round). White-tailed deer are seen throughout most of the tract. For a similar viewing opportunity, visit the Walton Tract: at the junction of Interstate 64 and VA PR 42 (Exit 29), travel north on VA PR 42 for about 10 miles to VA SR 632 on left, which leads to the tract. *NATURAL AREA WITH NO FACILITIES. PUBLIC HUNTING AREA: PLEASE CHECK WITH DISTRICT RANGER OFFICE FOR AFFECTED AREAS.*

Directions: *From Clifton Forge, southwest of Staunton, take U.S. Highway 220 south past Iron Gate and turn left onto VA SR 633 and follow for 2.5 miles. After crossing the one-lane bridge over Cowpasture River, the tract is on the left. Parking is signed as "U.S. Forest Service Walter L. Robinson Access Point."*

Ownership: USDA Forest Service (703) 962-2214
Size: 499 acres   **Closest Town:** Clifton Forge

The eastern cottontail rabbit occurs throughout the Commonwealth. Cottontails prefer more open habitats such as old fields and brushy edges.

ADAM JONES

SHENANDOAH

89

Description: Nestled along the West Virginia border in the Allegheny Mountains, Lake Moomaw was created in 1979 by the completion of Gathright Dam. Over 40 miles of shoreline, 2,500 acres of water, and thousands of acres of public land comprise Lake Moomaw.

Viewing Information: Several agencies administer land around Lake Moomaw. The U.S. Army Corps of Engineers constructed and maintains the dam, where a visitor center is located. The Virginia Department of Game and Inland Fisheries administers the 13,428-acre Gathright Wildlife Management Area on the west and east sides of the lake, while the USDA Forest Service manages 2 recreation areas on the lake: Coles Mountain (south shore) and Bolar Mountain (north shore). Gathright WMA is managed primarily for the production of wild turkey; chances are good of seeing the large bird. Listen for males, called gobblers, at dawn and early morning in early spring, as they beckon the females of their harems. Great blue heron can be seen year-round on the lakeshore; green-backed heron in the summer. Search for 3 species of owl (barred, eastern screech, and great horned) by looking for owl pellets under large pine trees. Excellent songbird viewing, especially in summer. Identify 4 species of squirrel: gray, red, fox, and southern flying (a nocturnal squirrel). In warmer months, snapping, eastern painted, and eastern box turtle are active, also black and water snake. *PUBLIC HUNTING AREA: PLEASE CHECK WITH DISTRICT RANGER OFFICE FOR AFFECTED AREAS.*

Directions: From Covington, take U.S. Highway 220 north for 2 miles to VA SR 687. Turn left and travel for 3 miles to VA SR 641, turn left. Travel for 0.5 mile to VA SR 666, turn right and travel 3.5 miles to VA SR 605. Turn right to dam.

Ownership: USDA Forest Service and others (703) 839-2521, (703) 962-2214
Size: 2,530 acres
Closest Town: Covington

Many wildlife viewers, especially birders, keep a list of wildlife species they have seen. These lists, often referred to as "life lists," can simply be a checklist of species seen, or more elaborate, including such information as the date, time, location, habitat type, weather conditions, and behavior of the animal. Taking field notes requires careful observation and aids in learning about different species and their habits.

Description: Interpretive nature trails, boardwalks, wildlife viewing blinds, wood duck nest boxes, an oak hickory forest, open grassy fields, and a Ducks Unlimited marsh with water levels manipulated to benefit wood ducks and migratory waterfowl provide numerous wildlife viewing opportunities.

Viewing Information: Over 100 bird species have been identified at Augusta Springs. In spring and summer in the marsh look for the wood duck, one of Virginia's most beautiful ducks. Males, or drakes, are more colorful than females (hens). In spring, it's possible to see a hen with ducklings. Identify the hen by the white eye patch and headcrest. During spring and fall migration, mallard, blue-winged and green-winged teal utilize the marsh, which also supports beaver, muskrat, and the blacknose dace, a silvery minnow with a dark lateral line. During spring, listen for spring peepers (a clear, single high-pitched note or "peep") and pickerel frogs (a low-pitched "snore"). Along the upland trail and field's edge look for ruffed grouse, American woodcock, wild turkey, and white-tailed deer, and in the evening, gray and red fox. Songbirds are abundant; obtain a bird list from the Forest Service.

Directions: From Staunton, take VA PR 254 9 miles west to VA PR 42. Travel 8.5 miles south on VA PR 42. Site is located at the north end of Augusta Springs off of Forest Road 1625.

Ownership: USDA Forest Service (703) 885-8028
Size: 50 acres   **Closest Town:** Staunton

The Augusta Springs Watchable Wildlife Area is an excellent site to see wood ducks. Pictured here is a male, or drake, wood duck.
JOE MAC HUDSPETH

SHENANDOAH

Description: Antebellum history, striking mountain scenes, and fine wildlife viewing merge along the lush valley of the Jackson River. Miles of trail offer viewing access to the river, hayfields, mixed hardwood forest, ponds, and wetlands.

Viewing Information: From late spring to fall, look for the belted kingfisher perched on a power line or hovering above the water, ready to seize an unwary fish. Kingfishers are easily identified by their big head, big bill, and headcrest. Females have brown breastbands; males do not. In winter, look for the white rump patch of northern harriers overhead or perched on a snag. From spring to late summer look for American goldfinch, ruby-throated hummingbird, indigo bunting, scarlet tanager, red-winged blackbird, and wood duck. Bald eagles are sometimes seen during winter/spring.

Directions: From Warm Springs, take VA PR 39 west for 1.4 miles to VA SR 621. Turn right and continue 1 mile, then turn left onto Forest Road 241 and travel 1.8 miles to area. Bear right at "Y" (campground on left) and follow road to parking area by river.

Ownership: USDA Forest Service (703) 839-2521
Size: 3,445 acres   **Closest Town:** Warm Springs

In summer, the male American goldfinch is easily identified by its brilliant yellow body, black wings, and black headpatch. Females have black wings, a green-yellow back, and yellowish underside. JOHN GERLACH

Description: A large, open field transected by a small stream and wetlands bordered by mature hardwood forests characterize this site. Wildlife plantings of autumn olive, lespedeza, and sawtooth oak enhance wildlife populations.

Viewing Information: Excellent for an uncrowded and more remote experience. The openness of the fields allows for good visibility. Spring and summer offer best viewing. Look for red-tailed hawk and American kestrel, white-tailed deer, belted kingfisher, woodchuck, cottontail rabbit, and many species of songbirds, reptiles, and amphibians. *NATURAL AREA WITH NO FACILITIES. PUBLIC HUNTING AREA: PLEASE CHECK WITH MANAGER FOR AFFECTED AREAS. ROUGH, UNPAVED ROAD TO AREA.*

Directions: *From Harrisonburg, travel west on U.S. Highway 33 for 9 miles. At junction of U.S. 33 and VA SR 612, turn right (north) and travel 9.5 miles (VA SR 612 changes roads - watch signs carefully). Turn left onto VA SR 817 and proceed for 0.75 mile. Make another left onto Forest Road 230 (unsigned) and travel 0.8 mile to fields.*

Ownership: USDA Forest Service (703) 828-2591
Size: 55 acres   **Closest Town:** Harrisonburg

Woodchucks, also referred to as groundhogs, are vegetarians, feeding on grasses, roots, stems, berries, and nuts. BILL LEA

SHENANDOAH

Description: Highland County, tucked against the West Virginia border, has the highest mean elevation of any county in Virginia. Dubbed Virginia's "little Switzerland," this mountainous, remote region is stunningly beautiful.

Viewing Information: Habitats here include extensive northern hardwood forests, red spruce forests, beaver ponds, and bottomland meadows along many streams. White-tailed deer are seen year-round, while black bear might be seen from April to December. During warmer months, many mammals might be observed: woodchuck, raccoon, gray and red squirrel, cottontail and New England rabbit, and snowshoe hare, with its summer rusty brown pelage and winter white pelage. Many songbirds nest and breed here in spring and summer, which comes late to this mountainous region. Several species of warbler, as well as cedar waxwing, solitary vireo, scarlet tanager, rose-breasted grosbeak, purple finch, and dark-eyed junco are among the nesting species. Look and listen for barred, eastern screech, and great horned owl in deciduous forests and forest edges, and saw-whet owl in the spruce-hemlock woods. Year-round resident hawks include red-tailed, red-shouldered, sharp-shinned, and Cooper's. In winter, look for rough-legged hawk and northern goshawk. One species stands above the area's diverse wildlife: a population of golden eagles graces Highland County in winter. Though it is rare, a sighting of this magnificent bird flying overhead near Virginia highways 640, 642, or 643 will be remembered for a lifetime.

Directions: From Monterey, travel north on U.S. Highway 220 for 7 miles to VA SR 642. Turn left and follow west to the West Virginia border. The viewing site is along VA SR 642 and many other roads intersecting VA SR 642, such as VA SR 640 and VA SR 634/644.

Ownership: Private and USDA Forest Service (703) 839-2521
Size: 45 square miles **Closest Town:** Monterey

In winter, Highland County is home to a population of golden eagles.
LEN RUE, JR.

WILDLIFE INDEX

The numbers following each species are site numbers, not page numbers. The listing represents some of the more popular species in the Commonwealth, as well as some of the best places to see them. This is only a partial list. Entries in bold denote a photograph.

WHERE THE WILD THINGS ARE

Falcon Press puts wildlife viewing secrets at your fingertips with our high-quality, full color guidebooks—the Watchable Wildlife series. This is the only official series of guides for the National Watchable Wildlife Program: areas featured in the books correspond to official sites across America. And you'll find more than just wildlife. Many sites boast beautiful scenery, interpretive displays, opportunities for hiking, picnics, biking, plus—a little peace and quiet. So pick up one of our Wildlife Viewing Guides today and get close to Mother Nature!

WATCH THIS PARTNERSHIP WORK

The National Watchable Wildlife Program was formed with one goal in mind: get people actively involved in wildlife appreciation and conservation. Defenders of Wildlife has led the way by coordinating this unique multi-agency program and developing a national network of prime wildlife viewing areas.

FALCON™